Architects and Firms

Architects and Firms

A Sociological Perspective on Architectural Practice

Judith R. Blau

The MIT Press
Cambridge, Massachusetts
London, England

This book was set in Baskerville by Village Typographers, Inc., and printed and bound by The Murray Printing Company in the United States of America.

Library of Congress Cataloging in Publication Data

Blau, Judith R., 1942–
  Architects and firms.

  Bibliography: p.
  Includes index.
  I. Architectural practice—Social aspects—
United States. I. Title.
NA1996.B55   1984   720'.68   84-11271
ISBN 0-262-02209-5

For Peter

Contents

Preface

There is an important social context in which the design and production of architecture takes place. This context includes the profession, architecture firms, clients, and practitioners' shared ideas about how buildings ought to look and ought to function. By and large most analyses of architectural practice have been historical or have examined the products of practice—the styles and the uses of buildings. Instead, I focus attention on the social underpinnings of design and production activities. The main theme of the book is that there are contradictory features in contemporary practice. They endanger the basis of architects' commitment and their collaboration; they create inconsistencies between architects' intentions and their accomplishments; and they generate inescapable dilemmas for firms that inevitably compete for design awards, commissions, and for sheer survival.

Of course, many scholars have dealt with the social history of the profession and of architectural practice. However, the focus has been on the most prominent architects or the critical events that have shaped the nature of the profession. Instead, I chose to investigate issues concerning the present, and I am interested in the great variability among many architects rather than the prominent and well known. For that reason offices were randomly sampled, and they exhibit great differences in many respects. The initial study was carried out in 1974, and it included 152 Manhattan offices and the architects who worked in them. After a severe economic recession a second study of the same firms was carried out in 1979 in order to explain how they generally fared and why some survived while others did not.

There are established interdisciplinary ties between sociologists and architects. They have collaborated with one another in user surveys and in neighborhood and community impact studies. Besides, sociologists, as well as psychologists and anthropologists, have carried out research on the interdependence between the built environment and the attitudes and behavior of people who work and live in that environment. This is research with which many architects are familiar. Such collaborative activities and research endeavors are motivated by humanistic concerns—to improve the quality of residents' lives and to enhance the urban environment. The reader who expects this book, written by a sociologist, either to add to our knowledge about the interrelationships between the built environment and people's attitudes and behavior, or to provide guidelines to professionals who want to improve the amenities offered by buildings, may be disappointed. This is because the research centers on the ways actual practice is influenced by its social context, not on how architects can ameliorate the social functions of buildings.

Indeed, the findings of this study indicate that most architects already want to give priority to the needs of users, yet the expression of that priority in built form is difficult to achieve, given the prevailing social and economic conditions. That is, architects' intentions to improve the usefulness of buildings are thwarted by multiple constraints—clientage, the market, and the organization of architectural practice. These constraints set close limits on the way in which practice can be carried out. Rather important shifts, it is inferred, would have to occur in the political economy of American society before there could be a fundamental change in the design of buildings so that they would better accommodate the psychological and social needs of users.

Although I assume that architects' intentions are thus shaped by the opportunities they have and the constraints with which they must contend, a similar assumption is not made about architectural design. Any cultural product, I assume, has an aesthetic character or style that has considerable autonomy and cannot be reduced to the social structures in which it is produced and embedded. Conventions that guide architecture as aesthetic expression are similar to those that guide the developments of music, the visual arts, and dance, and become incorporated into them. Such conventions are not very different in this respect from the conventions that underlie the way in which scientific knowledge is produced. Whether it is a novel design form, a new artistic statement, an important idea in science, each will make a dramatic impact in its own field and reshape the thinking of practitioners. This is not to imply that social norms, interpersonal influences, and the resources offered by organizations and work environments have no effect on the likelihood that a new "discovery" in each of these various fields will occur. After a creative discovery is made, however, it will become an integral part of a stylistic repertoire or a body of knowledge and will have long-lasting influence. That influence is independent of the initial facilitating social conditions. Thus, I do not assume that architectural styles are socially determined. Yet, because architects have different experiences, backgrounds, and different colleague relationships, their convictions about style and aesthetic merits of buildings do vary, and these convictions *are* socially patterned within the professional community. One of my purposes is to map these convictions and to examine how these patterns have consequences for the way in which practice is carried out in architectural offices.

How firm practice under ordinary times is altered by the conditions of dire economic straits is considered in the last chapter. The theme that there are structures of risk that arise from the contradictory features of practice and the profession of architecture are most apparent when we consider which firms fail, which firms barely survive, and which ones prosper during a severe economic recession. The legend of Daedalus provides the metaphor for the logic of the theme that structures of risk underlie the process whereby an initial contradiction unfolds to become advantage and disadvantage, success and ruin.

Acknowledgments

Certain portions of the analyses are reported in other papers of mine. Chapter 4 includes some of the materials used in "A Framework of Meaning in Architecture" from *Signs, Symbols, and Architecture,* edited by Geoffrey Broadbent, Richard Bunt, and Charles Jencks (Wiley 1980) and from an earlier paper with Hilary Silver in the *Quarterly Journal of Ideology* (Summer 1977). I also cite results that are in my article, "Expertise and Power in Professional Organizations," which was published in *Work and Occupations: An International Sociological Journal* (February 1979); and portions of a paper I co-authored with Katharyn Lieben, which appears in *Professionals and Urban Form,* edited by myself, Mark La Gory, and John Pipkin (The State University of New York Press, 1983), are incorporated into chapter 6. I am grateful to the publishers for their permission to use these analyses.

This book is not so much the reporting of research results as it is a reflection on some of the major findings of that research with an attempt to integrate them in terms of a middle-range theory that is of sociological interest and relates to the issues with which architects are concerned. The larger research project had a variety of objectives, not all of which are considered here. I must thank William McKinley who worked with me on another major portion of this study; his contribution played an important role in my rethinking later. The study began to take shape in 1973 and was concluded, with the final data analyses, in 1983. It thus spans several cohorts of students who helped with the interviewing, coding, and data analyses. I especially want to thank Mitchell Chamlin, William Cordes, Robyn Goldstein, and Stephen Light. The final draft of the manuscript was typed in Albany when I was in New York City, and I am grateful to

Kathy Brisley, Eileen Crary, and Mary Ann Strout, who efficiently and cheerfully coordinated this task.

Research support was provided by the Research Foundation of the City University of New York and by the Research Foundation of the State University of New York. Institutional facilities that provided space and resources are the Netherlands Institute for Advanced Study in the Humanities and Social Sciences, the Psychiatry Department of Albert Einstein College of Medicine of Yeshiva University, and the Center for the Social Sciences of Columbia University. I also want to thank my colleagues at the State University of New York at Albany for providing an environment that is intellectually challenging as well as highly congenial.

Without the cooperation of many hundreds of architects I would not have been able to write this book. It is impossible to thank every one of those who gave me special encouragement and advice along the way, but I owe a special debt of gratitude to those who provided guidance in the initial phase of the study. These include Leslie Goode, John Hagman, Frances Halsband, Alan Lapidus, George Lewis, Jan Pokorny, Robert Rotner, Richard Stein, David Swan, and Max Urbahn. James Morgan, senior editor of *Architecture Plus,* was especially helpful, as he generously devoted time to providing technical assistance with the language used in the questionnaires and interviews. Staff members of the American Institute of Architects were also helpful in providing information about firm practice.

It was the inspiring lectures of the late Professor Joshua Taylor that kindled my early interest in buildings and that provided me with the challenge of considering architectural practice from a sociological perspective. There are many sociologists who have helped me to nurture and sustain this interest, and among them I am particularly grateful to M. Craig Brown, Herbert Gans, and Magali Sarfatti Larson. Both Herbert Gans and Peter Blau read a late draft of the manuscript and helped me to clarify and communicate my ideas. Maintaining a proper balance in attempting to carry out a project that I hoped would be of interest both to practitioners and to academics was not always easy. To the extent that I was able to maintain this balance, I owe a great deal to the staff of The MIT Press.

My family knows how much I have appreciated their help. Reva's militant feminism helped to fuel her understanding when I worked on weekends, and she provided competent assistance with the index. Peter, though not such an unqualified feminist, has provided steadfast encouragement and, always, intellectual challenges.

Architects and Firms

1

The Daedalean Risk

Daedalus is remembered as the first to venture to fly. Fitting his son, Icarus, and himself with wings constructed of feathers attached by twine, wax, and glue to a light frame of wood, Daedalus and Icarus set out from Crete. What is often forgotten is that Daedalus, in legend at least, was also the first important architect, having designed the extraordinary labyrinth and temple complex for his patron, King Minos. It was Minos's pleasure and delight with Daedalus's architectural service that prompted Minos to hold Daedalus captive on the island of Crete, which was the reason Daedalus and Icarus risked escape with the artful wings.

This book deals with architecture as professional practice, as business, as occupation, and as a set of convictions about how buildings ought to look and function. Architecture in all of these respects is governed by structures of risk that accompany opposing conditions of various sorts. Risk is always conceived to be a situation fraught with hazards, but I use the concept of the structure of risk in a more specific way as well. The premise is that particular conditions contain an implicit contradiction that sets into motion processes that unfold to reveal the full implications of the initial contradiction while at the same time they create a resolution that in turn poses a new set of opposing conditions. The process develops inexorably in terms of its own logic.

The resolution of the predicament in which Daedalus found himself has a comprehensible and logical outcome: it clarified and decisively resolved the initial conflict, yet at the same time created a new problematic situation. Daedalus successfully escaped, but Icarus plunged into the ocean when the wax on his wings melted. To give another example from mythology, what led to Apollo's grievous loss of Daphne was that though he loved her, he was the God of the Sun and she a nymph of the cold-running waters. The very act of catching Daphne changed her, through Apollo's warmth, into a laurel bush. Thus any predicament governed by a structure of risk contains within it a contradiction that establishes a dynamic of transformation, and the resolution of the predicament both clarifies the original contradiction and establishes a new predicament. This literary principle of mythology serves as both metaphor and theoretical premise for this sociological study of architecture.

Specific ways in which the structure of risk operates are discussed throughout the book. A variety of forms of risk structure are inherent in architecture. These relate to the dilemmas that so prominently confront contemporary practitioners: the dependence on commissions, a poor distinction between architecture and building (and thus among architects and engineers, developers, contractors), the lack of congruence between those to whom the architect is ethically responsible (for example, the residents of a housing project) and those to whom the architect is accountable (the city agency commissioning it), the constraints imposed on design practice by the increasing size and complexity of architectural offices, the lag between plans and their fully realized built form. Another important dilemma is that architecture provides services that are not vital to people's health and welfare in the same sense that the professional services of physicians, or even lawyers and dentists, are. Many of these dilemmas result from the fact that much of the building field is controlled not by architects but by engineers, developers, and building contractors—at least in sheer numbers of buildings.[1] Economic fluctuations also create distinctive dilemmas for architecture. An economic crisis, as this investigation will show, while it creates general conditions of vulnerability, also makes it apparent which features of firms make them most vulnerable and their survival less likely than that of other firms.

Terms Defined

Built Form
Architecture as building has been of particular interest to the social sciences. The various ways in which buildings influence people's daily lives and attitudes has been an important topic for theory and research, contributing to social science knowledge

and having practical significance for architecture and planning. For example, William H. Whyte's (1980) investigation of how people use urban spaces, such as plazas and congested sidewalks, leads to some interesting conclusions about the order and rhythm exhibited by aggregates of people who seem to be merely disorganized crowds. Such conclusions are of sociological interest. Whyte's studies also have potential for application in the design of plazas and sidewalks for planners and architects concerned with the social values and utility of the built environment. In his 1967 study of Levittown, Gans finds that the shared driveways that planners had designed to encourage friendliness, in fact have the opposite effect when they become the battleground for disputes among neighbors' children. And Sommer's (1969) studies of bars, mental hospitals, and schools illustrate how the arrangement of physical space can encourage people to participate in sociable activities or hasten their withdrawal.

In contrast to the social science tradition that considers the effects of architecture on behavior is the tradition of historical scholarship that deals with the social and cultural significance of buildings. G. Wright (1981) and Hayden (1981) show how domestic architecture has reinforced cultural values concerning women's subordinate position in our society by the spatial design and location of houses. The broad links between cultural values and architecture have been made by a number of architectural historians, including Wayne Andrews (1947), James Marston Fitch (1947), John Burchard and Albert Bush-Brown (1961), and Lewis Mumford (1931, 1938).

And finally there are a host of investigations, including Gans's (1962) *Urban Villagers,* Jacobs's (1961) account of the nature of community in large cities, and White's (1980) book on the lives of Jewish immigrants in London's East End, that demonstrate how buildings and neighborhoods are used and modified in ways consistent with the cultural and class values of particular groups rather than with the intentions of planners and architects.

Although the principal concerns of this book focus on architecture as profession, practice, business, and conviction, architecture as building cannot be ignored since the prominence of firm practice rests on the evaluation of its projects, and the convictions of architects are more or less consistent with what is—or will be—built.

Architecture as Profession

The special meaning we attach to professional work relates to the wider division of labor in society, which has, as E. C. Hughes (1958:70) describes, moral significance. The "peculiar ambiguities with respect to what is seen as honorable, respectable, clean and prestige-giving as against what is less honorable or respectable, and which is mean and dirty" is what accounts for the differences with which various occupations (and the people in them) are viewed. In this moral sense—in the terms that Hughes defines professional work—architecture has the envied status of a profession. According to a general sociological definition of a professionalized occupation, architecture is grouped with a variety of other occupations with high standing, such as medicine, law, college teaching, the ministry, and engineering. The basis of the distinction between professions and occupations hinges on a number of characteristics.

One of these is the special expertise that professionals acquire through rigorous and long training that leads to certification or licensure. Architecture has been less successful than most other established professions in this regard. There are two observations worth making. First, as Cullen (1983) has demonstrated, architecture ranks relatively low compared with other professional occupations with respect to both educational requirements and percentage of practitioners who are licensed. The second observation, which in part can account for the first, is that architects have never agreed about the profession's core or specialized domain. The artistic and ideological foundations of the field justify architects' claim that they possess ecumenical proficiencies and knowledge. Vitruvius's position, that architects must acquire broad training and diverse skills, has not changed in its essence very much in two thousand years: "Let him be educated, skillful with the pencil, instructed in geometry, know much history, have followed the philosophers with attention, understand music, have some knowledge of medicine, know the opinion of the jurists, and be acquainted with astronomy and theory of the heavens" (quoted by MacDonald 1977).

Although the details of training and career obviously have a different cast today compared with Roman times, the eclectic and interdisciplinary features of architecture persist. Authors Henrik Ibsen and Ayn Rand, among others, have keenly seized on the point that architects' claim to exceptionally broad knowledge sustains a myth of the romantic hero with boundless vision and sagacity. In fact the profession continues to resist a definition of its boundaries and internal specialization. This is not so surprising, perhaps, considering that architecture in some measure is art, which is itself greedy in its jurisdictional demands, and in some measure it is applied science, which, unlike basic science, proceeds from the assumption of the interrelatedness of problems and solutions. Architecture stakes a claim to other competencies as well. MacKinnon (1965), an astute observer of the field, notes:

If an architect's designs are to give delight the architect must be an artist; if they are to be technologically sound and efficiently planned he must also be something of a scientist, at least an applied scientist or engineer. Yet clearly if one has any knowledge of architects and their practice, one realizes that it does not suffice that an architect be at one and the same time artist and scientist if he is to be highly creative in the practice of the profession. He must also to some extent be businessman, lawyer, advertiser, author-journalist, educator and psychologist. (P. 274.)

The professionalism movement in architecture has been based in part on the premise that interdisciplinary eclecticism is a major obstacle to the possibility of the profession's securing an exclusive mandate with respect to its preempted and preeminent activity: design. Starting perhaps in 1567 when Philibert distinguished the architect from the builder, the professionalism movement has attempted to give architecture a narrow and distinctive definition as a design field (although at times it has been contradictory in these objectives). (The details of this historical account are summarized in Jordy 1976; Kostof 1977; Jenkins 1961.) The internal divisions within the profession that are generated by forces for specialization on the one hand and eclecticism on the other have continuing significance for the profession and for practice. This is quite different from the situation that exists for most other established professions, which have marked an exclusive domain for themselves and within that domain have defined a variety of discernable specialties.

The attempt to secure an exclusive mandate over the affairs that pertain to a profession requires further clarification, for it is a second main feature of professional work. The claim to carry

out with indisputable superiority difficult work in the interests
of others is implicitly an imperialistic claim for such work. As
Freidson (1971:22) describes the contention for a mandate,
"The profession seeks the exclusive right to perform a particular kind of work, control training for and access to it, and control the right of determining and evaluating the way the work is
performed." Success in establishing that mandate leads to a
monopoly over services and a market that is controlled by the
profession.

Ministry and law and, later, medicine, dentistry, nursing, and
teaching were largely successful in what Larson (1977) calls the
dual project of professionalization. These fields were able to
define a market for professional services and to establish monopolistic control over it. The corollary is that these professions
used their clients' dependence as a means of attaining social
status and concrete economic and social privileges. Why architecture has been historically unsuccessful in this dual project has
been traced by Larson in a more recent essay (1983). Her conclusion is that the success of a variety of other professions—
engineers, interior designers, speculative builders—in vying
for the same market has undercut the ability of architecture of
attaining a monopoly, and hence has reduced the likelihood of
achieving the social status and income comparable to those of,
say, medicine.

Professionals have clients, and the history of clientage and
how it relates to what and how architects design and build is a
central topic of many historical analyses (see, for example, Kaye
1960; Andrews 1947; Pevsner 1936). From the nineteenth century on, with the decline of the traditional patronage system,
competition for state and private contracts intensified the tension between the definition of the architect whose chief responsibilities were to design and art (and perhaps, it was also
hoped, to history) and of the architect whose chief responsibilities were to the client. This tension took several forms.
Architecture as art could be defended on traditional grounds,
whereas pleasing the client was alleged to mean cutting corners,
using cheaper materials, and emphasizing the practical over
the sublime. The other side of the argument is that above all
architecture is utilitarian; the highest priority is that the building
serve the best interests of the client. This split is drawn in several ways, but Jenkins (1961:188) draws attention to one im-

portant component of it when he contrasts the "tact, acumen, and above all, the persuasive polish which is readily associated with the 'professional man'" with "the creative talent." In the decades following World War II the split in architecture had become three-way, with the artist contrasted to the professional and with the two of them contrasted to the architect who designs for users and whose interest is in a more humane environment—not art, not the client, not savings. We will examine the extent to which these three professional models are salient in architecture and the extent to which they figure in practice.

Another putative component of professionalism is the notion of equality among professionals. Having similar backgrounds and having undergone the same training and credentialing, professionals make up communities based on collegiality and trust (see Goode 1957). These contemporary patterns originate from medieval institutions; the promotion to master craftsman put the journeyman on an equal footing with his former teacher. Yet few architectural practices in modern times—the Comasco group and to some extent the Architects Collaborative, and Team X—actually advocate equality, although most unfailingly stress the importance of collegiality. The compromise of equality is due in part to the recognition that although professionals may be equal, artists cannot be. It is also related to the imperatives of organization. The conditions under which there is less inequality and when individuals are likely to exercise voice in matters of importance is examined in chapter 2.

Professionals work long hours, marry late, have few children, and postpone retirement; vocational commitment to a calling is a main component of a professional career. In part this is the case because the initial choice of the field entails a professed zeal and dedication, but also, as Becker et al. (1961) have shown, the process of socialization incurred in training (to say nothing of the role of psychic investment, time, and money) helps to promote identification with the chosen career. Shared symbols and language within the profession and an emphasis on success that is unique to that profession all tend to reinforce high commitment. The fact that professional work takes place in organizational settings, however, matters a great deal, and organizations are more or less successful in sustaining and channeling commitment.

Architecture as Practice

The term *professional practice* is easily taken as an oxymoron, as much so as *bureaucratic art*. But the complexities of project design require organized practice just as the playing of much classical music requires a symphony orchestra. For orchestras economic reality and bureaucratic rationality dictate uncontroversial programs at the cost of innovation and experimentation (Arian 1971). Architectural practice is not so very different.

Practice as Process

In all offices, large and small, architecture is a process, an ongoing set of activities involving tasks that are specialized and at the same time interrelated. The distinction between architecture as an efficacious art and other arts in this regard was made by Wotton (1961:1) in 1624: "As in all other Operative arts, the end must direct the operation." There is a great deal of variation among firms with respect to the way they organize that operation. In some firms work is subdivided into a number of distinct tasks, and each person carries out a different operation; in other firms the operation is consolidated and the process relatively undifferentiated. But Wotton had more to say about the end; it is, he said, simply "to build well." And, he continued, "Well building hath three Conditions: Commoditie, Firmness and Delight" (1961:1). These terms still have wide currency; architects now refer to "habitability," "good engineering," and "visual pleasure."

All practicing architects endorse in principle all three conditions, but there are wide differences among them as to which have priority and how they relate to the mechanics of office practice. For this reason, plus the fact that each new project is a unique case, the practice of architecture appears to be an ad hoc process. The uniqueness of each project, the distinctive qualities of every client, the idiosyncratic character of each award jury, the lack of control over such uncertainties as the conditions and costs of construction, new complexities of building regulation and financing, and the sheer problems of maintaining groups of people who can work well together all contribute to the makeshift character of architectural practice. Yet such practice is not mere improvisation. The negotiations that appear ad hoc and the way in which a firm handles the unique and the uncertain are governed by a structure of constraints and opportunities that reflect its organizational configuration and economic character. There are also structures of risk that develop out of internal contradictions and the external demands on firms by their environments. These too are systematic rather than random. The views of architects about how buildings ought to look and to function are also not happenstance but have a meaningful pattern that can be deciphered.

Practice as Organization

Practice can be seen from one perspective as an office consisting of a set of positions occupied by individuals. This refers to distinctive structural arrangements commonly called organizations. Few architecture firms are as large and bureaucratic as many other organizations with which we often deal—banks, hospitals, universities, chain grocery stores—but they share with all organizations a number of important characteristics. Organizations are defined by W. Richard Scott (1981:9) as "social structures created by individuals to support the collaborative pursuit of specific goals." He explains that all organizations, because they confront a number of common problems, share the same generic characteristics: "All must define (and redefine) their objectives; all must induce participants to contribute services; all must control and coordinate these contributions; resources must be garnered from the environment and products or services dispensed; participants must be selected, trained, and replaced; and some sort of working accommodation with the neighbors must be achieved" (p. 9).

What is instrumental for the solution of these various problems is a more or less formalized structure characterized by a division of the organization into subcomponents, the designation of supervisory responsibilities, assignment of tasks, routines for communication and coordination, and a set of technologies. Once established this formalized structure has consequences independent of the intentions of those people who work and collaborate within it. For example, a large organization nearly always has more subdivisions and greater formality than does a small organization of the same type, regardless of the level of skills of the workers and regardless of what sort of organization workers want.

Architects are more concerned with the process of design than with the organizational basis of design, yet by abstracting structural elements from the firm's organization and its activities, it is possible to capture important elements of that process and also the larger matrix in which that process takes place. For example, the ways in which joint ventures are negotiated is of no concern in this study, but the fact of having such linkages with other professional firms is of interest, for regardless of the way in which they are negotiated, the joint venture has important consequences for other firm characteristics.

Practice as Business in a Market Economy
Unable to secure a monopolistic control over building, architecture is extremely vulnerable to economic fluctuations. This vulnerability is the source of continual controversy over what professional firms can and cannot do to keep a foothold in the market without jeopardizing professional ethics and integrity. That such market practices as the production of stock plans, investment and mortgage services, and development work generate the controversy they do indicates the economic pressures on the profession, as well as the salience of a design identity (Gutman 1983).

Since the time of ancient Egypt, the architect in precapitalist societies had been associated with the powerful and rich elite (Kostof 1977). This hardly entailed a position of unquestioned security or even one of autonomy, but precapitalist elite sponsorship ensured the legitimization of a uniform aesthetic and typically the recognition of the architect as a design generalist. A particular aesthetic style symbolized the power of the secular ruler or church, thereby giving the architect reflected repute and, except for the Middle Ages when the architect was both designer and craftsman (Gimpel 1961), the architect's task involved most aspects of design, as well as the supervision of its execution, but not the execution itself.

In a capitalist economy the imperatives of the market establish and limit the options for client and professional alike. Because firms need clients, commercial objectives become important, if not dominant, in the firm's activities. As Burnham so frankly stated, "My idea is to work up to a big business, to handle big things, deal with big businessmen and to build a big organization, for you can't handle big things unless you have an organization" (quoted in Sullivan 1926:285–286).

One imperative of the market is specialization in the interest of efficiency; another is, as Burnham put it, large size; another is an internal organization that has a more or less bureaucratized structure; and a final one is economy of means. The contradiction is that market imperatives are antithetical to those of elite artistic traditions. Such assertions as Geoffrey Scott's (1914) that architecture must place "beauty over order," Summerson's (1963) admonition for an "aesthetic synthesis," and Moholy-Nagy's (1946) defense of a "perfect balance between feeling and intellect" all attempt to deny the contradiction and provide a justification for a contemporary architecture that asserts aesthetic ends, not merely accommodates an economy of means. For a time it seemed that a solution to the contradiction was impossible; the international style, which fostered monotony and repetition, dominated building design for nearly fifty years. Yet as Banham (1980), Jencks (1981), and others have proclaimed, modernism has been replaced by a proliferation of styles, by novelty, and by competing ideologies. From a socioeconomic point of view, this development is not surprising: competition among the units of a market economy—whether between clients or between architectural firms—in the long run will result in diversity as the aim is to capture a special niche—a symbolic monument for the client or a unique stamp for the firm.

The firm's special style, which stands behind the forms of the buildings it designs, is one question. Another, which is not totally unrelated, is the success in designing buildings that meet prevailing quality standards. My findings highlight an unusual conclusion: the structurally perverse firms (I call them eccentric) are highly successful in this regard.

In contrast to the conclusions concerning competition for recognition for design merit, in the competition for economic advantage, there is a structural process whereby some firms are cumulatively advantaged and others cumulatively disadvantaged, leading to a bifurcation of firms and their markets. The success of some firms in securing large corporate commissions can be contrasted with the necessity of other firms to scramble for small commissions. The evidence presented in this analysis suggests strong contrasts between a set of firms that constitute the monopolistic core of architectural services and a set that comprise a more competitive periphery. The extensive literature on economic segmentation of this sort deals exclusively with industrial rather than professional firms, but this study confirms, with certain important modifications, the relevance of economic segmentation in the practice of architecture too.

The basic principle of dual economy theory is that firms in the economic core tend to be large, have high profit margins, internal labor markets (different career ladders), high qualifications for workers, high wage rates, and product diversification. Firms on the periphery tend to be small, have low profit margins, rudimentary internal labor markets, low worker qualifications, low wages, and lack of diversification (Averitt 1968; Edwards 1979; Tolbert, Horan, and Beck 1980; D. M. Gordon 1972; Beck, Horan, and Tolbert 1980). Although this theory posits a somewhat simplified distinction, its virtue is that it focuses attention on an underlying principle that results in observed economic inequalities and thus explains them. The tendency of architecture firms to exhibit core or peripheral characteristics and for them to deal with core or peripheral clients is central for an understanding of their success as businesses and, in an unexpected way, for an explanation of their probability of failure or survival.

Architecture as Conviction
Whatever language is employed—feeling (Langer 1966), codes of meaning (Bonta 1980), intentions (Norberg-Schulz 1963), morality (Scruton 1979), deep structure (Broadbent 1980)—architects can be said to have convictions about how buildings ought to look and function. In *From Bauhaus to Our House,* Tom Wolfe (1981) drew attention, in a somewhat caustic fashion, to architectural ideologies, maintaining that they center on matters of mere fashion and avant-gardism for its own sake. Current styles grow out of rebellion against the bourgeois, he argues, yet they also reflect a profound contempt for the client. His views have some support. Frampton (1980:10) writes, "The vulgarization of architecture and its progressive isolation from society have of late driven the discipline in upon itself. . . . At its most intellectual this tendency reduces architectonic elements to pure syntactical signs that signify nothing outside their own 'structural' operation."

This point of view—that architectural conviction and creation have become highly insular and exclusory of societal needs—can be contrasted with an alternative one—that architects have abdicated their own artistic convictions and independence to elite demands and commercial interests (Fitch 1947; Gowans 1970; Tafuri 1980). In chapter 4 I examine the convictions of rank-and-file architects and conclude that neither point of view is correct; architects have neither succumbed to art for art's sake nor is their economic dependence on clients matched by an ideological identification with them. Rather their ideological convictions are more progressive, aesthetically and socially, than is generally realized, and the obstacles for their realization lie in economic and organizational sources.

Professional architects not only bring conviction to design, but in attempting to manage the uncertainties of practice, they establish priorities on the basis of conviction. Convictions of practice, however, differ from convictions of design in that the former are more pragmatic, rooted in the economic realities as well as the social relations of the firm. In chapter 4 these convictions of practice are described, and in chapter 5 the question of their efficacy is discussed.

Concepts and Theoretical Assumptions

Contradictions

The Daedalean risk refers to those instances in which structures of risk are likely to affect firms with certain characteristics and the people who work in them. The general explanation for such structures is sought in a set of contradictions generic to contemporary architecture generally. From the standpoint of individual practitioners these structures of risk are perceived most often as particularistic dilemmas or unique situations. The result is attributed either to fate—bad or good luck, poor or fortunate timing—or to individuals—a clever decision, an unwise personnel policy, a creative personality. The point here is that regardless of luck, timing, or individuals, the broader structural conditions of risk can explain why some firms are more profitable than others, are more likely to be recognized for their design accomplishments, or are least likely to fail in bad times.

In contrast to the uniform and linear trajectories that characterize noncontradictory processes—for example, the transformations typically observed in fetal growth, aging, and the development of a new technology—contradictory forms generate opposing outcomes. Just as a structure of risk can lead to ruin, it also contains the seeds of success because it is a basic configuration for challenge and a creative response. Contradiction is the precursor of failure and success as it simultaneously generates unique opportunities and formidable dangers. The story of Daedalus has both a tragic and an accomplished end.

Historically contradictions constitute the structure from which the dynamics of the dialectical process are generated. Central to both Hegel and Marx is the principle of dialectical change. While for Hegel the historical process was driven by the conflict between abstract ideas, for Marx the contradictions inherent in relations of production and the very nature of the economy are the mechanisms for social change. There is no effort made here to examine long-term historical change or to weigh the relative merits of Hegelian and Marxian theory, yet this important philosophical dispute informs the analysis that I undertake. I identify those circumstances in which the intentions (abstract ideas) of architects are inconsistent with social and material conditions and other circumstances in which intentions are rooted in conditions in which they are consistent. It is not the strength or even the coherence of the set of intentions that determines whether they are consequential but rather their initial relationship to social and economic conditions.

In addition to the conflicts between ideas and social and economic conditions, another form of contradiction is between the conditions themselves. Two examples, by analogy, illustrate the point. Marx maintained that contradictory economic conditions contain the seeds for change and transformation. For example, capitalism must continue to expand because the very growth of capital depends on new markets. But according to the laws of surplus labor (whereby workers give to capitalistic enterprise a portion of their labor), workers become increasingly impoverished and, eventually, local, and finally foreign, markets disappear. A very different instance illustrates in a simpler way how a contradiction has its own dynamic properties that cannot be inferred from the properties of its elements alone. One main advantage of steel lies in its capacity for compression and another in its capacity for tension. Yet when steel is stressed by reversals of compression and tension, it loses its potential superiority derived from each property, becomes fatigued, and fails.

The Daedalean risk is hardly different from these examples of contradiction and of the newly emergent forces that the contradiction sets into play, yet the Daedalean risk draws attention to the actors too. The contradictions built into the conditions of the profession and practice of architecture are beyond the control of architects, but the consequences that ensue from opposing conditions disclose opportunities, however briefly, for response. Thus, in employing the concept of contradiction, I call attention to the impersonality of the social and economic factors involved in particular problems confronting practice and the profession, but the term *Daedalean risk* clearly implies that an element in the resolution of a contradiction is the possibility of inspired choice.

Rationalization

As a major historical process that has profoundly altered values and the organization of work, rationalization involves the principle that all matters ought to be judged in the terms of objective evidence and be justifiable on rational grounds— indeed on the grounds of efficiency. This orientation conflicts with the transcendental criteria of evaluation in art and supports the utilitarian criteria of the marketplace. According to Max Weber (1976), rationalization achieves the subordination of the sacred to the profane, of the charismatic to the rational. Simultaneously it involves a process of structural transformation; it incorporates Adam Smith's (1937) principle that a comprehensive division of labor among workers and among enterprises promotes economic efficiency and growth. In the domain of work this involves the substitution of personal control by formal authority, the standardization of products through processes of routinization, and the careful calculation of the relation between means and ends. Confounding and furthering this process are the features of corporate capitalism. As capitalism advanced, its earlier entrepreneurial goals of capital accumulation became transformed into those involving control of markets through monopoly and then oligopoly, with its greater emphasis on the control and standardization of labor. The extraordinary specialization achieved in twentieth-century work far exceeds the earlier conceptions of the division of labor. The worker has now become, as Braverman (1974:179) puts it, a "mechanism articulated by hinges, ball-and-socket joints, etc."

Professional organizations themselves are not yet so fully rationalized as industrial firms, nor is the professional worker engaged in such highly routinized work as Braverman describes. Nevertheless large corporate architecture firms begin to take on many of the features of their corporate clients and use the same strategies to control their markets and their employees. The deskilling phenomenon is not rampant, but it is common enough. One architect I interviewed in a prestigious

Park Avenue firm had started work with the firm over fifteen years before and for the past ten had done nothing but door moldings. "My options of moving elsewhere," he told me, "are limited."

The concept of rationalization is a bridge linking the convictions of architects, the profession of architecture, and practice, for whether its primary source is ideological (as it is according to Weber) or embedded in the nature of economic institutions (as it is according to Smith), the principle has profound significance for work of any kind.

The Study

This investigation is based on a survey of 152 Manhattan architectural firms (listed in the appendix) and over 400 architects who work in them. In order to examine how firm practice changes over time, I collected two sets of data, the first in 1974 and the second in 1979. The 152 firms are a representative sample of Manhattan offices (selected randomly from the Manhattan telephone directory); they constitute about one-third of all Manhattan firms (of which there were approximately 540 in 1974).[2] Undoubtedly they are not typical in many respects of firms throughout the country. New York City firms, for example, are preeminently design oriented. Except perhaps for Chicago, Manhattan offers the architect the best possible environment: an aesthetic vanguard, a wealthy clientele, professional architecture schools, and a diversity of professional organizations that are used for consulting, subcontracting, and joint ventures.

In the first study information about each firm (its characteristics as an organization and as a professional practice) was obtained in a one- to three-hour interview with a principal of the office: the owner of the firm, a partner, or the president. Because most of the information I was seeking was factual, considerable variation and flexibility was built into the interview format. Sometimes an assistant was called into the office during the interview to provide specific information from the files; on occasion the information sought was not available at the time and was obtained later in a telephone call or by letter. For the approximately 60 firms that had fewer than six architects, a telephone call, usually about an hour long, supplemented by a short questionnaire, was generally used instead of a personal interview.

Although this format was somewhat complicated for data collection, it was ideal for obtaining factual information about an organization because it was flexible and targeted knowledgeable sources. It was not adequate, however, for securing other data, such as the priorities of leadership or managerial strategies. For questions of this sort, therefore, it was important to obtain information from a principal in a face-to-face interview. This was not possible for small firms in which there were no personal interviews, and for that reason the investigation of certain issues dealing, for example, with the overall philosophy of firm practice (its agendas), is based on fewer than the total number of firms. There are also characteristics of firm organization, such as the complexity of its formal structure, that are relevant only for comparatively large practices; the analysis using such characteristics is based only on firms with at least six full-time architects and a complement of technical staff.

In 1974, the time of the first data collection, I was told repeatedly by architects that in spite of a decline in the economy, they would never leave New York. But the economy continued to worsen, and the decline in the construction industry began to have serious repercussions for local architecture. The fiscal crisis of New York in 1976 dealt the most severe blow for it meant the end of much building activity directly or indirectly financed by the city or the state. By 1979, when the second study took place, nearly half of the original firms had failed.

The second round of data collection was not as extensive as the first, for its main purposes were narrowly focused: to determine what features differentiated firms that failed—had gone bankrupt or had left the city—from those that had not and to analyze major changes that surviving firms had experienced. In 1979 the data collection was based primarily on telephone interviews, although for the largest firms questionnaires supplemented interviews to obtain detailed information pertaining to number of personnel and annual productivity. The response for both studies was extraordinary; there were only a few refusals in 1974 and none in 1979.

A second source of information is the individual architect. In 1974 the person in the firm who had been interviewed was asked if questionnaires could be sent to the architecture staff. In about two-thirds of the firms, permission was given and the names of individual architects supplied so that I could send each a questionnaire. The reluctance of many of the firm heads to divulge names of staff or to encourage their participation is understandable, though it creates problems of representativeness and of the generalizability of the findings based on individual data. Fortunately such refusals were not systematic—that is, the head's likelihood of refusing was not related to such firm characteristics as type or size—and the inevitable refusals by individuals were not systematic either—that is, related to their position in the firm or to other firm characteristics. Overall about 50 percent of all the architects in the 152 firms returned questionnaires. Thus although these data are a valuable source of information, some caution is necessary in generalizing the results obtained from these data, particularly when dealing with questions of architects' convictions.

Method of Inquiry

Classic studies with which social scientists and many architects are familiar are based on the investigation of a single case—a psychoanalytical analysis of a youngster (Freud's analysis of Little Hans's dreams), a group (the working-class gang whose ways of coping are interpreted by William F. Whyte in *Street Corner Society*), a neighborhood (Gans's *The Urban Villagers*), or an entire society (Benedict's *The Crysanthemum and the Sword*). Such detailed and thorough investigations of a single case yield not only a Gestalt, a richly detailed description of that unique instance, but suggest by implication a more universal explanation—about dreams, social relationships, or a society's cultural values. The principles inferred presumably apply not merely to Hans or Japan or one neighborhood but to all that are similar. An investigator who focuses on a particular case draws attention to how the various elements are interrelated and mutually reinforcing. The West Enders' acquiescence to Boston redevelopers and the destruction of the community (described by Gans) are the outcome of a general process that depends on the fatalistic attitudes of the urban villagers, their closely knit peer groups, their lack of ties to the world outside the community, and the paternalistic attitudes of those who traditionally provided social and other services. A sensitive and skilled researcher provides through such a synthetic analysis an understanding of a coherent whole and of the underlying dynamics.

The advantages of a case study are simultaneously its limitations. A guiding theoretical assumption is that elements (people or groups) constitute a social system and that features of those elements (group values, individual attitudes, social class, methods of child rearing) are interrelated and can be subsumed under a broad interpretative framework. This makes it difficult to account for incongruities and variation. Moreover it is impossible to tease out what is a genuine causal factor that operates on others. Is it, for example, the high social density, the ethnic homogeneity, the traditions of respect instilled in early childhood, or the tendency to repress aggressive feelings that is responsible for the strong norms of deference and politeness among the Japanese? One cannot find the answer to this question in *The Chrysanthemum and the Sword*. The relative importance of cultural values and of social class cannot be disentangled to explain why the West Enders failed to organize to save their neighborhood. And one could entertain other hypotheses for Little Hans's dreams of the horse besides a losing battle with his father over his mother's love.

Because this investigation is not based on a case study, it does not focus on processual features and the distinctive qualities of a given firm, a group of professionals, or any particular practice of architecture. Rather than attempting to paint a single ideal type of contemporary architecture, I am examining variations among firms and within them in order to explain these differences. Such an objective requires a study based on many cases, which is the reason for basing the analysis on surveys of many firms and architects. Such comparative data capture the variation for which I use statistical analysis, which is important because the range of variation among architectural firms is great. A final reason for a survey is that this approach has certain inherent advantages in establishing systematic comparisons with an end to explaining causal relationships.

Everyone is familiar with empirical relationships cast as causal statements: proximity increases the likelihood of friendship; social support buffers the effects of stressful events; spatial arrangements in an office reinforce attitudes about status differences among workers; dome structures are unusually stable owing to the action of the meridians that carry loads down and of the opposite action of the parallels at the top and the bottom to, respectively, shrink and elongate.[3] All of these empirical, causal statements follow from systematic, comparative observations of many cases, not just one. They are typically cast as probabilistic, not deterministic, influences. To use the example about the stability of dome structures, there is not a perfect mathematical function (to the architect's peril) that can relate the forces because not all relevant other influences can be considered absolutely constant. The weight and quality of the brick and mortar will play some role; distortion of the structure is caused by uneven settling and by winds; the proportions of the dome affect its stability. In short we are talking about systems of variables that are not isolated and about systems in which many more variables than can be measured are operative. These are variables that ideally we would want to control—either experimentally or by randomization—or to measure.

Experiments are ideal for establishing causal relationships because randomization can be used to eliminate unknown sources of causation, because the causal (independent) variable(s) can be manipulated by the experimenter, and because the effects of other extraneous causes can be ruled out, as in the case of the sterile laboratory or a vacuum chamber. Moreover in fields in which the experimental method has been used successfully, such as nuclear physics and inorganic chemistry, the potential for accurate and refined measurement is great.

Social scientists, however, seldom use experiments, for reasons that render the approach practically useless. There are ethical problems in manipulating subjects or lying to them; it is impossible to study large-scale phenomena in experimental settings; many things of interest in the social sciences exhibit much initial diversity (with respect to, say, individuals' residence or their criminal backgrounds). It is precisely for these reasons that experiments are not very useful for the purpose of generalization, and besides that there are the problems of accurate measurement in contrived situations. For these reasons, the approach adopted here is probabilistic.[4] Two points should be made. First, as a substitute to randomization, the typical social science survey is based on a sample that is representative of the population and therefore leads to results that are generalizable. Second, some of the sources of variation that are canceled out through randomization in an experiment are deliberately measured in a social survey and, once measured, can be statistically controlled and entered into the causal model. For example, if it is found that architects, compared with members of other occupations, are more likely to be Democrats than Republicans, it may be useful to control statistically for the size of the city in which they grew up (since we know that in the general population, those who grew up in big cities tend to be Democrats and those from small towns, Republicans). We may find that the reason why architects tend to vote Democratic is that most come from large cities and that otherwise architects are no more likely to be Democrats than any other occupational group. On the other hand we may find that controlling for the size of the city of origin makes no difference, and architects, regardless of where they grew up, are more likely than people in other occupations to vote Democratic.[5]

The conclusions of this study are based primarily on regression and discriminate function analyses, and both incorporate these principles of probabilistic influences and of causal effects that are independent of other conditions. Readers interested in the details of these analyses are referred to chapter notes. The main findings of the study and the interpretation of these findings are reported in the text, and their discussion will present no particular difficulties for those unfamiliar with statistical procedures.

2

Voice

In the private industrial sector the tripartite division of owners, managers, and workers is rooted in economic factors. Social relations among these groups are governed by their respective relations to capital, the means of production, and the commodity of labor. The fact that workers sell labor subordinates them to owners and also to managers to whom control of the production process is delegated. Workers have virtually no voice in company affairs and are powerless to influence decisions that affect their daily working lives.

Whereas economic relations of production constitute the primordial source of inequalities in voice—the exercise of power over one's own work, over the work of others, and over the allocation of resources—the means by which these inequalities are sustained are organizational in nature. Administrative elites in the public sector secure a monopoly of control comparable to that of managers and owners in the private sector, and workers or employees in both sectors occupy a similar position of powerlessness. Why inequalities that stem from economic conditions in industrial and commercial enterprise are mirrored in state and public bureaucracies is a topic of current interest and debate, but the issues involved would take us far beyond our concerns here.[1] Pertinent, however, are the organizational means by which control is achieved. In both the public and private sectors these means are bureaucratic and relate to the rationalization of work: standardization of routines, subdivision of work into its simplest components, hierarchical coordination, formalized communication, and regulation through rules, directives, and detailed procedures. In industrial work these organizational means of control are supplemented by technological means of control—the automated assembly line and the computer providing the prototypical examples.

Private professional offices are also organized around the principles of capital, the means of production, and labor. And they are also more or less rationalized to accord administration control over work and certainty in operations. Yet cleavages in power and influence are not so great. For a variety of reasons professionals have more autonomy and are more likely to exercise some voice over decisions than most other white- and blue-collar workers. The sheer complexity of tasks is a major reason that professionals of all ranks usually have some voice; the ethos that emphasizes both voluntarism and egalitarianism is an additional reason for the influence of professionals. In architecture the belief that creative work requires a high degree of discretion and freedom from bureaucratic constraints further increases the opportunity for autonomy and voice for every trained architect. But in practice this belief is tempered by the division of responsibilities and the fact that some architects engage in work that is considered more creative than that of others.

Nature of Power

Complexity of Work
Rank-and-file workers are alienated and powerless not because of the high degree of specialization that accompanies the subdivision of a complex task but because of the form that specialization takes in industrial enterprises. Subdividing a complex task into a variety of minute specialties with no complexity retained at the final subdivision results in boring and meaningless jobs. This system also promotes inordinate control over workers. Owners and managers are responsible for the initial subdivision of tasks, and they alone control the means to supervise and coordinate the diverse tasks and product components.

The rationale for such excessive specialization and fragmentation originates with Adam Smith but was most clearly articulated in 1832 by Charles Babbage. He provides an example from the manufacture of pins whereby the work of a single craftsman is subdivided into seven components: drawing wire, straightening wire, pointing, twisting and cutting heads, heading, tinning or whitening, and papering. The cost to the owner would be halved, Babbage suggests, by replacing the craftsman with seven unskilled specialists. Techniques of deskilling labor were advanced even further at the end of the nineteenth century by Frederick Taylor (1911), who perhaps has had the most direct and lasting influence on management strategies adopted in the twentieth century.[2]

Some types of jobs resist deskilling more than others. Truck driving, child care, firefighting, and farming do not require much formal education, but they are jobs that exhibit integral diversity and therefore are difficult to simplify and routinize. There are other occupations, such as teacher, architect, anesthesiologist, and engineer, that also exhibit a diversity—they require a grasp of complex and interrelated knowledge—that makes them difficult to routinize. Professional jobs entail learning what others consider to be riddled with uncertainty and indeterminacies. As a result professionals exercise considerable discretion over tasks, play a key role in the evaluation of their own performance, and have exceptional autonomy in the organizations in which they work. But this does not make professional work immune from deskilling in any absolute sense. Organizational rationality is found to undermine the scope of professionals' theoretical and operative knowledge; this is reported in studies of priests and ministers (Benson and Dorset 1971), computer programmers (Kraft 1977), engineers (Perrucci and Gerstl 1969; Crozier 1964), filmmakers (Faulkner 1983), lawyers (Smigel 1964), and college teachers (Heydebrand 1983b).

Surely there is a prophetic ring to Babbage's plan for implementing a division of labor among mathematicians to convert the French numerical system into a decimal system after the French Revolution. That division entailed a hierarchy of mathematicians, with the top level responsible for the formulas and the bottom responsible only for the routine arithmetic. With technological developments, Babbage foresaw the time when each hierarchical level could be replaced—one by one, starting at the bottom—by an increasingly sophisticated machine. The complex knowledge of the intellectual or the professional worker provides some protection from fragmented specialization, but that protection is hardly complete.

Ethos of Voluntarism and Egalitarianism
Accompanying the importance of training and specialized knowledge for the likelihood, though not the certitude, that

professionals will exercise some voice in their organizations are the professional values of voluntarism and egalitarianism. Because one implies the other, they are considered together. Similar training, common work experiences, and the shared recognition of how mastery is acquired and exercised provide a basis for social bonding among the members of any group of professionals who work together. In addition there is a close fit between particular organizational objectives and individuals' professional goals, and typically, at least in architecture, the owner or partners have the same general training and background as employees. In certain respects architecture offices have the qualities of what Becker (1982) describes as a collective enterprise bound together by a set of common conventions that overrides the implications of a division of labor and differences in power. Collegiality, the extent to which goals are shared, and a set of common conventions all contribute to and reinforce the ethos of egalitarianism: the belief that equal voice in professional affairs is just and proper.

To the extent that egalitarianism is recognized as a key value in firm practice, so is voluntarism, which rests on the principle that individuals have the skills and good sense to act more or less autonomously when they can, to consult with others when they cannot, and to organize their own work and carry it out. Thus the principles of voluntarism and of egalitarianism are complementary; together they encourage participation and freedom to exercise voice.

The same values that tend to support firm democracy also have had deplorable consequences. Any organizational form (whether it be the profession as a whole or a firm) built on bonds of trust and compatibility that stem from members' similarity tends to promote distrust of people who are different. Specifically it results in discrimination and distrust of those who are in some way different. New staff, I was often told by architects, are hired because they will be congenial and will fit in; they should be people with the same ideas or a similar philosophy. It is not surprising that most offices have few or no minority staff, and female architects are hired primarily to design interiors. Of the offices in this study, only two had a female principal in 1974.[3]

Artistic Integrity

All professional work is complex, and the principles of voluntarism and collegial egalitarianism are more or less evident in
any private professional setting, including law firms, large medical group practices, and offices of certified accountants. But the
essence of architecture is that it centers on creativity. Ask the
architect:

> *Stubbins:* A complete solution involves many facets. In truth
> architecture is an approach towards life. It is a social art.
> (Quoted in Heyer 1966:218.)
>
> *Wright:* Architecture is that great living creative spirit which
> from generation to generation, from age to age, proceeds, per-
> sists, creates, according to the nature of man and his circum-
> stances as they both *change. That* really is architecture. (Wright
> 1953:311.)
>
> *Kahn:* Design is form-making in order
>   Form emerges out of a system of construction
>   Growth is a constructive force
>   In order to creative force
>   In design is the means—where with what when
>   with how much
>   (Kahn 1960:169.)

The architect-designer demands latitude for judgment and
artistic freedom of expression, which must be exercised, to be
sure, within the limits imposed by the client, the character of the
site, the cost of construction, and materials. In art generally the
ideal has historically emphasized artists' opportunities for freedom and the absence of artificial restrictions. This has been
affirmed by rationalists, such as Kant (1790), systematic philosophers, such as Ross (1982), metaphysicians, including Whitehead (1978), and even by neo-Marxists, such as Marcuse (1978)
and Althusser (1971). Architecture is not pure art, yet architectural design requires artistic creativity. As sociologist Brewer
(1972:4) states, "The choice among the many possible designs
that might be technically and functionally satisfactory must be
left to the discretion of the architect. Norms of artistic integrity
are clearly central to the conception of architecture as art as well
as a purely utilitarian profession. Without the ability to consis-
tently exercise aesthetic choice in their work, architects would

be incapable of producing recognizable or identifiable styles of design."

Nevertheless in office practice not all architects are designers; the traditional subordination of apprentice to master architect still carries some currency; the leading designer is often so imbued with charisma that the chances for junior architects to express their design skills become thwarted (see Andrews 1947: 252–287; Christopher Jones 1970; Moore 1970; Caudill 1971; Winklemann 1973; Rock 1973). Even Walter Gropius (1962: 79), head of one of the first collaborative architectural ventures, TAC, writes, "Individual talent will assert itself quickly in such a [collaborative] group. . . . Leadership does not depend on innate talent only, but very much on one's intensity of conviction and devotion to serve. Serving and leading seem to be interdependent."

Firm Attributes
Generic characteristics of the profession and practice of architecture together tend to promote relatively wide participation. These include the complexity of the work, the ethos of egalitarianism and voluntarism, and the link between creativity and autonomy. But factors that operate to maximize architects' opportunities for exercising voice in the affairs of their firms are variable rather than constant. Some architects are more specialized than others, and not all architects have design responsibilities.

There is also variation among firms that can be expected to affect how much influence architects, collectively or individually, exercise. Some firms have a wide scope of services; in this case the opportunity for participating in decisions may be greater compared with firms with a very narrow scope of services. Also it is probable that people have less influence, on average, in a very large firm than in a small one. If power is distributed in an absolutely equal way, every individual in the small firm will have greater voice—proportionally, that is—than every individual in the large firm. Yet there are somewhat more complicated reasons why power not only tends to come in smaller allotments on the average but also in less equal allotments in big than in small organizations. The far greater resources in large organizations provide management with incentives to centralize control, and even though there are compelling reasons for management to decentralize many decisions to the bottom level (because of the sheer volume and complexity of tasks in a large organization), the increasing length of the hierarchy creates a reverse bottleneck effect: decisions of consequence are constricted at the level of middle management (P. M. Blau and Schoenherr 1971).

Accommodation to bureaucratic features is not unusual for professionals in organizational settings. In fact bureaucratic structures provide a protective barrier for professional endeavors. They shield staff physicians from administrative details and paperwork, insulate university faculty from a myriad of student affairs unrelated to teaching, and protect architects from tasks that range from balancing the books to involvement in boring technical routines (see Larson 1977:184; Smigel 1964; Palumbo 1969; Kornhauser 1963; Perrucci 1971). Yet bureaucratic features, notably formalization through rules and regulations, also encroach on the discretionary powers of professionals. When formalization is substantive, dealing with tasks that professionals view as their exclusive prerogative, rather than procedural, professionals feel depreciated and are resentful (G. Miller 1967; Hall 1968).

Another form of rationalization, one clearly linked to management's interest in financial savings, is the expansion of the nonprofessional technical staff to achieve a reduction in the professional staff. Besides achieving savings, however, an increase in the numbers of technicians also results in subdividing some architectural work into simpler routines that the technicians can perform. Such decisions as these—to increase the relative numbers of engineers, draftsmen, or technical workers—usually signal a new emphasis on production at the expense of design.

Surely one of the factors that is concurrent with the rationalization process is the passing of time. As firms become older, routines become more entrenched, innovation less likely, decision making more perfunctory. In general the ossification of firms with age (Liebert 1976) can be expected to erode the collective exercise of voice.

Also relevant to an understanding of the conditions under which professionals exercise voice is the contrast between the traditional firm, owned by a single architect or by a partnership, and the incorporated firm. The principle of corporate organization is the vesting of control of operations in a specialized management to eliminate administrative and operational uncertainty and to deal with the contingencies of an uncertain and competitive market (Chandler 1962; Melman 1951; Braverman 1974). Although incorporated professional firms are different from incorporated businesses in that capital accumulation is dampened by their reduced investment opportunities, they are similar to businesses in that a major purpose of incorporation is the protection of capital by means of a comprehensive system of control that emphasizes technical-rational criteria of decision making over substantive criteria.[4] This is achieved by depoliticizing decision issues and by increasing the dependency of the middle- and low-ranking professionals on top decision makers.

These observations dealing with the interrelationships between the nature of professional work and the characteristics of firms guide the investigation of how much voice architects have, collectively and individually, in the decisions of their firms.

Collective Voice

A way to discover how much voice individuals exercise in the affairs of their organization is to ask them about the influence they typically have over a variety of issues critical to decision-making areas. Each architect was asked whether she or he had some, little, or no influence over decisions in six areas: hiring professionals, assigning professional responsibilities, making changes at the initial stage of a project, making changes at the final stage, approving the design, and selecting a contractor. For the analysis of collective voice, the sum of individuals' scores was divided by the number of responding professionals.[5]

Several features of firms are expected to affect collective influence, and these are included in the analysis. How generalized or specialized is the work carried out by professionals is indicated by the average number of distinct tasks (out of a total of twenty-three) in which architects report they have responsibilities.[6] The complexity of the firm's work is measured by the number of comprehensive services provided to clients.[7] Total size is measured by number of personnel.[8] Formalization, a prime indicator of the extent to which the firm's practice is bureaucratic and rationalized, is measured by the number of procedures governed by written regulations.[9] The relative separation of production from design (and also the extent to which some architectural work has been routinized) is indicated by the percentage of the total staff that are technicians.[10] Firm age is simply the number of years since the firm was founded, and incorporated status is reflected by two measures: whether the firm is incorporated and whether the firm is affiliated with another corporate entity. The use of engineering consultants, the final factor considered, is expected to affect collective voice adversely for several reasons.[11] Firms that use consultants are dealing with a more complex organizational environment than those that do not, and this is generally found to concentrate power in the hands of top managers (see Zald 1970; Salancik, Pfeffer, and Kelly 1978). Also the tendency of firms to develop their production capacity at the expense of architectural services can be evident in the expansion of their technical component (which is already considered) or in an increase in the use of outside technical consultants.

The results of the analysis can be simply summarized: practically all of these factors reduce collective power. For example, the greater the size of the technical staff, the less the collective influence of architects. Parallel results are obtained for formalization, firm age, incorporation, affiliate status, and the use of consultants; each reduces the voice that the average architect has in the firm. But the real reason why this is the case has to do with the size of the firm.[12] Compared with smaller firms, large ones have more formalized rules, are older, have a higher proportion of technicians, are more likely to be incorporated or be an affiliate of a corporation, and to have engineering consultants. It is the case, for example, that in offices with large proportions of technicians, architects are granted less power in decision making, but the only reason why this is the case is that large offices tend to have both substantial numbers of technicians and centralized power structures. By itself the relative size of the technical component has no causal effect on collective voice. Sheer size has powerful consequences; it completely explains why the other factors considered are negatively related to collective voice though they have no causal negative effect on voice. That is, these statistical relationships disappear when size is controlled.

To clarify with another example how a statistically controlled variable can explain a relationship between two other variables by making that relationship disappear, I can refer to the classic case of variation in Swedish fertility.[13] It is observed that in Swedish towns with many storks there is also a higher birthrate compared with Swedish towns with fewer storks (table 2.1). But the inference that storks bring babies, in spite of the empirical association between them, is generally believed not to be correct. Indeed if one breaks down all Swedish towns into ones of different sizes, there is no statistical relationship between storks and the birthrate within towns of the same size; the relationship vanishes if one controls town size. (This is shown in table 2.2.) It is the case that small rural towns have high birthrates and also many more storks, while large cities, such as Stockholm, have low birthrates and very few storks. Similarly given a certain size level, there is no association between formalization and the extent to which power is shared, but small firms do have few rules and a wide distribution of power, and large firms have many rules and a narrow distribution of power. Thus firm size explains why there is more centralization of power in corporate firms and less in partnerships and sole proprietorships, just as the size of Swedish towns explains why fertility is high in places where there are many storks and low in places where there are few storks.

Two other factors affect collective voice even after size has been taken into account: the wider the scope of the firm's activities and the more complex the tasks of individual architects, the greater will be the collective influence of architects. Office size also plays a role here.

Table 2.1
Swedish towns with stork populations and birthrates

	Few storks	Many storks
Low birthrate	95%	10%
High birthrate	5	90
N	100	100

Table 2.2
Swedish towns of different sizes, stork populations, and birthrates

	Small towns		Big towns	
	Few storks	Many storks	Few storks	Many storks
Low birthrate	4%	6%	100%	90%
High birthrate	96	94	0	10
N	3	90	97	10

Office Size

Size has a strong dampening effect on the collective exercise of voice. It does so directly by reducing the average portion of power a person has. It also accounts for why offices that are more fully rationalized—both organizationally and in their economic structure—are less democratic. Indeed these are the larger firms. Yet the extent to which work is complex—both at the level of the firm and at the level of the individual architects—expands collective influence. Because size plays a role here too, the discussion is organized around figure 2.1, which clarifies the relationships.[14] This figure shows the causal influences; each arrow depicts an effect independent of the effects of the other factors in the model (specifically these other factors are statistically controlled).

Size has a substantial negative effect on power. In large firms architects participate much less in decision making on the average compared with architects in small firms. This is evident in figure 2.1 by the direct negative connection (A) between size and collective voice. Thus regardless of how specialized or complex the tasks of individual architects are, the opportunities that architects have of influencing decisions are much greater in small firms than in large ones.

Large size also has another negative effect on collective voice, which is indirect. In large firms individuals carry out fewer tasks; this increasing specialization simultaneously reduces their influence (the product of line B and line F is negative). This negative effect operates over and above the direct negative effect. Thus, large size cumulatively, directly and indirectly, disadvantages professional architects.

Paradoxically although large size reduces individuals' influence, it also indirectly increases it. This is because size has two

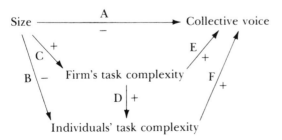

Figure 2.1
Analysis of collective voice

indirect paths or effects that are positive: (C times E) and (C times D times F). First, large size expands the complexity of the firm's tasks (its comprehensive services), which in turn increases participation in decision making. Second, large size, because it increases comprehensive services, broadens the opportunities for architects to engage in a greater variety of tasks and thus indirectly expands their power. But overall the sum of the negative influences of size on collective voice (taking the direct and the indirect negative effects into account) is much greater than the sum of its positive effects.

These results are a portent for the democratic practice of architecture; the reason has to do with a fundamental dilemma. The wider the scope of the firm's services and the less specialized individual architects, the greater will be the collective exercise of voice. Yet because of the contradictory effects of size, these two features are generally incompatible. In principle the most participatory firms would be those in which many comprehensive services are offered and those in which architects exercise discretion over a variety of diverse tasks—that is, they are not very specialized. Yet large offices exhibit the first feature, and small offices exhibit the second. Few firms have both features.

One question that follows from these findings is whether the consolidation of managerial control that accompanies an increase in firm size is realized in economic or other gains. If we ask why managers in any enterprise do not actively promote participation in decision making, the answer usually is couched in terms of "efficiency" or the "distinctive knowledge required for administration" or the "prerogatives of those with capital investments."

Individual Voice

Managers, Designers, and Staff Architects
Having discovered that architects' mastery of diverse tasks generally is positively and directly related to their influence, it is important to determine whether this holds at different levels of the firm—more exactly, whether everyone's power is augmented by wide and complex responsibilities or only that of some is. The approach to this problem is to categorize all architects by position: managers (owners, partners, and associates),

staff designers (employees who have primarily design responsibilities), and staff architects (employees who engage in the
more technical professional work, such as detailing, drafting,
and writing of specifications).[15]

The overall difference in their influence is considerable. The
average values for the answers to the questions are 9.4 for
managers, 5.5 for designers, and 3.4 for other architects. Managers, not surprisingly, exercise the most voice in decisions and
staff architects the least. We have already found that diverse
tasks on the average increase collective voice. In fact when we
look at individuals in different positions, work in diverse tasks
increases the voice of managers far more than it does the voice
of employees.[16] The greater the involvement of a manager in
most of the twenty-three different areas, the greater will be the
manager's power. And managers with a narrow scope of involvement in them have comparatively little influence.

These are the areas that constitute the core of professional
work. Economists Kenneth Arrow (1974) and Frank Knight
(1956, 1965) maintain that what makes managers distinct from
rank-and-file workers and eminently powerful is the fact that
they contend with administrative and environmental uncertainties. Centralized power, according to these economists, resides in the fact that managers deal with the risks of competition,
pricing, litigation, and market contingencies. Although I cannot dispute the notion that a source of managerial power is
dealing with such uncertainties, I do contend that a main source
of managerial power in the professional firm is monopoly over
domains of work that are intrinsically professional—not managerial nor even entrepreneurial—in nature. Thus a main
source of centralization in architecture firms is the appropria-
tion of domains of ordinary professionalized competencies.

Esoteric Knowledge

The expert deals in a matter-of-fact way with issues that are
esoteric for the layperson. Professional expertise implies that
knowledge and skill with respect to matters within the profession's domain are taken for granted. They are, in fact, quite
routine. What is not at all routine within the field is any area of
uncertainty that lies at its boundaries or beyond them, in adja-
cent fields or in the newest specialties in which few are trained.
A distinction is made here between work in core areas (which is
found to be important for managerial power) and work in fields

at the periphery, fields that are considered by the profession to be esoteric and recondite.

Every architect was asked about her or his competence in eleven such areas. These were considered in 1974 to require skills outside an architect's traditional training, to be especially difficult, or to require special experience. These areas are: complex structural systems, complex mechanical systems, complex electrical systems, acoustics, lighting design, landscape design, special materials, experimental structures, prefabrication, alteration of existing structures, and restoration and preservation. The total number of areas mentioned provides an indicator of the person's command of the esoteric.

For both staff designers and staff architects competence in these nonroutine fields that require special knowledge and training substantially increases their power. This is not the case for managers.[17] This connection between power and possessing knowledge of what others view as being highly uncertain is not new in the sociological literature. As James Thompson (1967: 127–136) makes clear, those who cope with uncertainties in organizations are more likely to be consulted by others and to exercise influence in decision making (see also Hickson et al. 1971; Hinings et al. 1974). When dependencies of top-ranking staff on lower-ranking staff are rooted in the superior knowledge of the latter, realignments in the exercise of voice can be expected. Power, as Emerson (1962) defines it, is rooted in other people's dependence.

Thus the extent to which individuals exercise voice is both positional and epistemological. Managers have the most power; the findings indicate they monopolize influence and control the affairs of the firm through involvement in most or all core activities of professional practice. Other architects have less power, although designers have more than the staff architects. Yet for both designers and staff architects, the more knowledgeable they are of esoteric specialties, the greater will be their opportunities for exercising voice in the affairs of the firm.

This serves again to remind us that specialization plays a different role in architecture than in the other established professions. The clear branches of knowledge and practice that divide the fields (within, for example, medicine and engineering) have never emerged in architecture. In the absence of specialty-based power, low-ranking architects are likely to find that abstruse knowledge is the bargaining chip to secure the dependencies of management, and high-ranking architects establish monopolies over the broad core of professional knowledge to maintain organizational control. In this way the lack of clearly defined specialties in the profession of architecture obscures the sources and nature of power.

Voice and Organizational Outcomes

Politics of Participation
Once ensconced, power tends to be accepted and legitimized, and there is a common perception that mutuality of interests is served. Yet when the distribution of power is questioned, the very fact of conflict of interest at once raises political questions. They are political, as Kaplan (1964:12) uses the term, "in that broader sense which includes every group and perhaps every personal relationship insofar as questions about the acquisition and the exercise of power arise." Always the questions dealing with increasing members' participation and power are political in nature: When the others get more, how much do we lose? Why have equity of power when some incur the most risks?

Architecture firms are more democratic than industrial and commercial establishments because they are professional organizations. But the same issues derived from political theory are relevant for all organizations, professional or not, in considering the relative merits of widening the exercise of voice.

There are three arguments against expanding opportunities for voice, each with a distinct set of assumptions. One argument emphasizes that differences in power are equitable and just; another conceives power to be a win or lose situation; the third is that inequalities are necessary for the sake of efficiency and effectiveness.

The first position assumes that some people are more responsible (or more creative, or better educated, or have risked more of their capital) compared with other people (who are lazy, or less well educated, and so forth). From the assumption of initial inequalities follows the conclusion that some deserve more power, the others less. Eckstein (1966:237–238), for example, argues that economic institutions must be run in an authoritarian manner since rank-and-file workers have neither the capabilities nor the talent to participate in decision making.

The second argument, that power is a limited resource and one's gain in power accompanies the other's loss, resides in the conception of zero-sum resources. Whenever power or economic resources are hotly contested, political language is often couched in the zero-sum concept as a slogan for fundamental change. As such it is a useful construction of reality and an effective rhetorical device. At the same time it provides those in power with the personal justification for not relinquishing any power whatsoever for fear that less power means loss of the monopoly.

Of course, there is a particular type of encounter that never can have other than a zero-sum outcome. These are often dyadic in nature; examples are two-party political elections, a tennis match, a poker game. Personnel decisions and career advancement in organizations are sometimes cast in the terms of a zero-sum game as individuals vie for the single promotion or a raise. And when boundaries are drawn between two groups of workers (management versus union), the relations of conflict often polarize and become a zero-sum outcome.

The third argument is based on the position that hierarchical distribution of power is more efficient and leads to a more effective organization than any alternative. Differences in power is the pragmatic means to coordinate the work of people carrying out different tasks and to ensure that responsibilities are assigned and that quality control is maintained through supervision. This is the position taken initially by Adam Smith and Max Weber and argued most stridently by Babbage and Taylor.

Before confronting these issues empirically, the assumptions that motivate these arguments ought to be examined. First, taking the argument for initial inequalities, it is possible to turn on its head the assumption that a person ought to have the power she or he deserves. As Simmel (1955) indicates, in any given social arrangement, say an organization, the attribution of deserving qualities is merely deduced from position. Simmel's (1950:150) conclusion, "The position makes the man," summarizes two important premises. The first premise is that the opportunities and experiences that accompany a position of importance educe skills and talents (1908:685–687; 1955:141–152). The second is that the virtual capabilities of everyone are initially equal, but when a collectivity makes more or less arbitrary distinctions, all sorts of reasons can be supplied to justify the inequalities that result (Simmel 1950:300–303). In short it is the fact of having power or of filling a position that creates capabilities, not the other way around. Supporting this notion are the laboratory studies in which the experimenter randomizes the distribution of status; those whom group members are told are the best informed, the leader, or the most talented are perceived in that way, and individuals who are assigned high status act in ways congruent with the expectations that accompany high status (Rosenthal 1968; Berger, Rosenholtz, and Zelditch 1980).

In contemporary organizations contention for resources is structured as a zero-sum game in the sense that there may be only one position to be filled and more than one applicant and in the sense that workers can be split along any one of various dichotomies (management versus employees, management versus union, white collar versus blue collar). Yet many have argued that this is not generic to organizations but rather a transient circumstance in the historical development of Western organizations (Rothschild-Whitt 1979; Pateman 1970; Clegg and Dunkerley 1980; Mandel 1975; Lindenfeld and Rothschild-Whitt 1979).

Unlike economic resources that have a substantial zero-sum quality (on which liberal economists, including Lester Thurow, and conservative economists, such as Milton Friedman, tend to agree), there is nothing that resides in power that makes it restrictive to a zero-sum solution. For example, Tannenbaum et al. (1974) find in a study of industries in a variety of socialist and capitalist societies that when the power of workers is greatly expanded, the power of management does not decline. An understanding of how this happens comes from the work of Kanter (1977) and Rothschild-Whitt (1979): an increase in the complexity of each person's work broadens responsibilities and at the same time increases the interdependencies throughout the organization. And because interdependency is the sine qua non of power, mutual interdependencies empower all participants. My own investigation of a large psychiatric hospital (Blau 1980; Blau and Alba 1982) indicates that organizational democracy can be achieved through the sheer complexities of interdependence that result when every person has multiple responsibilities in a variety of domains. Under these circumstances psychiatrists listen to nurses' aides and take their opinions into account, and aides' respect for the clinical skills of psychiatrists is enhanced. Such a complex structure expands power and the accompanying responsibilities because staff members become mutually dependent allies.

The last argument against enlarging participation is based on the pragmatic premise that organizational effectiveness and efficiency depend on hierarchical coordination. Simmel (1955), who makes the argument that virtually everyone is qualified, also makes the most convincing case for power differentiation and hierarchy. The question he asks is, Would there not be chaos were there not differences in power? One line of response follows my reasoning: coordination can be achieved by means of complexity when people are interdependent. The second line of response is in the form of a query and is as pragmatic as the argument: is expanded participation in contemporary organizations a serious impediment to their efficiency and effectiveness? As Pateman (1970:108) notes, the human results (the moral and psychological well-being of employees and workers) of participatory organizations are shown to be unequivocally better compared with hierarchical organizations, but the conclusive argument ultimately depends on considerations of economic efficiency and effectiveness.

Efficacy of Collective Voice
In some firms junior architects are free to call the client to discuss the project; in other firms junior architects are free to call the office of the zoning commissioner to find out restrictions on a site. A key to understanding power is to know that some issues considered trivial by management are organized "out" of the bonafide agenda whereas those viewed as important are organized "in" that agenda (Schattschneider 1960:71). To deal directly with the efficacy of greater voice in matters of importance, it is necessary to examine structured opportunities for power in critical areas of firm practice. When staff help to influence decisions that in fact have been organized "out" by managers, staff may feel responsible, but it is not the same as being in a position to determine the outcome or to make the decision; this effect is what Verba (1961:200) calls pseudo-influence.

I attempted to identify critical tests of participants insofar as they deal with items that are always organized in the agenda for an architecture firm and also indicate positions of power that give ongoing opportunities for influence. There are three such indicators:[18]

1. Total number of positions accompanied with the power of having direct contact with the client.

2. Number of individuals who typically (on an average-size project) share responsibility for the project.

3. That someone other than the principal can be in charge of a project.[19]

There are seven indicators of the firm's effectiveness as a professional organization and its economic efficiency:

1. Number of design awards received from 1969 through 1973.

2. Average evaluation of a firm's projects by approximately thirty faculty at New York City architecture schools.[20]

3. Client repeat rate (percentage of clients that commissioned more than one project from 1969 through 1973).

4. Client referral rate (percentage of clients in 1975 that commissioned a project on the basis of a client's recommendation).

5. Profitability (percentage of projects from 1969 through 1974 with construction costs of at least $1 million).[21]

6. Productivity (number of projects completed in 1973).

7. Staff commitment (average score for staff members on a set of items concerning satisfaction with work and career).[22]

The critical test is whether expanded participation impairs performance. I examined twenty-one relationships (a matrix for the three factors of participation and the seven factors of performance). Office size, which has an influence on the likelihood of participation, is also related to performance measures. Thus size must be held constant so that any effects that size may have on the relationships between participation and performance measures will be removed.

The overall answer to the question concerning the effects on performance of expanded opportunities for the exercise of voice is fairly clear: firms in which there is more participation tend to perform somewhat better than firms in which there is less. The majority of the partial correlations are positive; eight of the positive ones are of sufficient magnitude to be fairly confident that they are genuine, not chance, findings. A few of the relationships are negative, and two are of sufficient magnitude to consider them important, though these two negative ones are just barely significant. The substantive results based on the positive relationships can be summarized:

• The more positions there are in which individuals who fill them have the power of direct client contact, the higher tend to be experts' evaluations of project quality, the higher is the client repeat rate, and the higher is the proportion of projects with construction costs of at least $1 million.[23]

• The more individuals who share responsibility for a project, the higher is the client repeat rate and the higher is the percentage of projects with construction costs of at least $1 million.[24]

• The more likely that someone other than the principal is in charge of a project, the higher tend to be experts' evaluations, the higher is the client repeat rate, and the higher is staff commitment.[25]

There is some negative evidence, however. There are two relationships that, though small, are significantly different from chance and thus suggest some qualifications to the overall conclusion.

• The more individuals who share responsibility for a project, the more likely is the firm to receive few awards.

• The more likely that someone other than the principal is in charge of a project, the lower is the client referral rate.[26]

The general conclusions are that by and large the fact of wide opportunities for exercising power in important decision areas in architectural practice improves firm performance. While stipulating two exceptions to the generalization, it can be stated with some confidence that for firm performance more voice is better than less.

The two exceptions are interesting for they lend some credence to a store of traditional lore in the profession. Some architects told me that clients like to feel they are dealing with the head of the firm in all matters related to the project. While the results that deal with this matter of client contact are in direct opposition to the beliefs of these architects, clients apparently do get somewhat ruffled if the head of the firm is not solely in charge of their project: they do return, but they do not send their friends. The subdivision of project control and its negative relationship with award winning is an issue of somewhat greater complexity, and it relates to the peculiarity of the structure in high-quality firms, an issue that is taken up later.

Conclusions

Architecture offices are either private or corporate enterprises and as such assume many of the characteristics of all other money-making establishments: subordination of employees to managers, rationalization of the firm's activities and of its internal division of responsibility, and administrative control over the means by which work is produced. Yet these offices (and other professional organizations) have attributes in direct opposition to the principles of capitalist enterprise: each architect is trained to carry out highly complex work, the professional ethos of voluntarism and egalitarianism, and the value attached to artistic autonomy. The tension within architecture between economic constraints and professionalism makes questions about voice fundamentally important, and the answers help to clarify why some offices cope better than others with the contradiction.

Initially it was discovered that firms that are most rationalized along both organizational and economic lines are more highly centralized than traditional professional firms. The reason for this is systematic variation in size. Routinization, standardization, and corporate control, which many architects view as having pernicious consequences for the quality of their work, are not directly responsible for centralization of power, though such factors as these do accompany centralization. The reason is that these factors of rationalization accompany increases in size, but they have no effect in and of themselves on whether many or few exercise voice. Only their large size accounts for why the most rationalized firms are centralized. Although size, on the average, reduces the amount of power that individuals have, it has two contradictory consequences: large firms have many complex tasks (comprehensive services), and that increases decentralization, but large size promotes individual specialization, and that brings about centralization.

A second issue is why some individuals have more voice in decisions than others. Largely this is the result of positional differences: managers have greater voice than designers, and designers have greater voice than other architects. In part managers monopolize influence by exercising control over the core of architectural practice, whereas design and staff architects gain influence through their understanding of esoteric fields. In contrast to the broadly based comprehension of all facets of professional work that managers employ to establish and maintain control over firm affairs, what extends employees' influence is specialized and recondite knowledge. Thus what erodes monopolies of power can be understood in epistemological terms: it involves comprehensive knowledge and mastery in new areas that senior professionals consider enigmatic. It is the dependence of managers on staff with expertise in peripheral areas that empowers lower participants.

This interpersonal and political process is conceived to be a fundamental and distinctive component of the architectural profession precisely because of the absence of recognized specialties. In most other professions positions of status and power are granted those with the most exotic field of specialization—the neurosurgeon, the high energy physicist, the constitutional lawyer—whereas their counterparts in more broadly based fields—the internist, the solid state physicist, and the lawyer in general practice—rely on the specialized experts.

Variation in participation among individuals has a number of consequences for firm performance. Architecture offices are not democratic; some (see Winkelmann 1973) consider most offices to be run autocratically. Yet they do vary in the extent to which opportunities for participation are open to many or to few. The results of my analysis indicate that more voice is better than less for the performance of the firm. The wider the participation in major items on a firm's agenda, the more likely it is that the firm will do superior work. The negative evidence against this conclusion is not trivial, but it weighs little against the much stronger positive evidence.

There are contradictions between the more or less traditional features of architecture, such as its fundamental morphogenesis as art, and the newer features of firm practice that relate to rationalization of work and managerial control. This contradiction is necessarily absorbed within any contemporary architectural practice, and most comprehensively so in firms with pretensions of being design firms, which is what most of the Manhattan firms in the study aim to be. Yet the extent to which voice in decision making is decentralized, notwithstanding the odds against it given the contradiction, is efficacious for the practice of the firm. How the preservation of voice affects architects' zest for work is dealt with in the next chapter.

3

Commitment

Just as architecture is not mere building, architects are not mere professionals. Architecture has its place in religious imagery (Solomon's temple, the tower of Babel), in every center of power (the Hofburg in Vienna and the Louvre), in war (the Trojan horse, moated castles, and, I might add, the vulgar conceit of defensible architecture in U.S. cities), and in literature (*Northanger Abbey, The Castle,* and the *Colossus of Marousi*).[1] Most important, buildings are commendatory or not in terms of standards of beauty, aesthetic pleasure, and expression. It is no wonder that architects profess to be artists.

I asked each of the 422 architects, "What are the distinctive qualities of architects compared with people in other professions?" The vast majority (98 percent of all architects, including those with technical responsibilities as well as designers) gave answers that in part or in whole dealt with art and creativity. Some focused on creativity that is synthesizing in nature, whereas others dealt with the personal and individualistic qualities of creativity. Architecture is viewed to have holistic features because "a person can combine art with science"; "many problems can be solved creatively—problems that are technical, social, visual, spatial"; "the architect works with highly diverse problems to produce a new solution each time." Others emphasized the individualistic character of creativity: "design involves personal expression"; "architects can be very independent in how they develop their ideas."

A number of architects mentioned personality characteristics that reveal the self-concept of the artist. Some presented a heroic image of the architect: "they are romantic"; "architects are visionaries." Another image encompasses traits that verge on the eccentric: "architects have a bigger ego than most"; "they are difficult to get along with."

These responses are not surprising. Architecture does select for such personality characteristics as creativity, self-expression, and eccentric individualism (M. Rosenberg 1957; MacKinnon 1962; Schmidt 1973), and schools of architecture reinforce them (Carmon and Mannheim 1979; AIA 1973). The temperaments of some of the best-known architects in the history of the field, such as Frank Lloyd Wright, and of designers portrayed in literature (Howard Roark in *The Fountainhead* and Solness in *The Masterbuilder*), provide exaggerated support for such characteristics as defining the role of the architect (see Saint 1983).

Architecture as Art

The conception of architecture as art is not new in the chronicles of building. Evidence suggests that although the special standing of Egyptian architects rested initially on their craft skills, later it rested on their special intellectual talents. That of Greek architects was defined increasingly in terms of creativity (Giedion 1971:7–9; Hauser 1951, 1:33, 52, 117). The notion of genius, however, emerged most prominently in the Renaissance (Hauser 1951, 2:70–76; Wölfflin 1963:201–224), although there is evidence that even during the Middle Ages, high value was placed on the creative imagination of architects in spite of their anonymity (van der Meer 1967; Gimpel 1961; see especially von Simpson 1962:62–90).

Almost since the beginnings of civilization, architects have thus considered themselves to be, in large part, artists, and they have been so considered by others. What is new in the twentieth century is the diffusion from the visual arts to architecture of the concept of the avant-garde and, along with it, art for art's sake. There is some disagreement as to when exactly this occurred. Tafuri (1980:98) traces this reconceptualization of architecture to the Bauhaus, "the decantation chamber of the avant-garde"; Michael Kirby (1967:233), a sculptor and Happenings producer, also views the Bauhaus as particularly critical for the avant-garde because of the intense interaction among diverse types of artists. Giedion (1971:6, 266) suggests that architecture was linked with the avant-garde when it became defined as sculpture and credits Corbusier's 1933 Swiss Pavilion as the main point of departure. Yet these were European developments. Referring specifically to the U.S. architectural scene, Burchard and Bush-Brown (1966:323–325) argue that the concept of art for art's sake permeated architects' unconscious views for about two decades, until 1958, when Yamasaki brought it into the open by boldly proclaiming, "The social function of the architect is to create a work of art." At this point building purpose—civic, social, political, religious—and the criteria of efficiency and function become indisputably subordinated to design aesthetics. The tenor of the period is perhaps best illustrated in the statements of leading design architects:

Louis Kahn: A social plan is an arrogant plan. One has to make a distinction between a way of life and a way of living. One is general, the other is personal. (Interview in Cook and Klotz 1973:183.)

I. M. Pei: Architecture really is the need to synthesize the best out of life. (Interview in Diamonstein 1980:161.)

Richard Meier: Architecture is high art. (Interview in Diamonstein 1980:106.)

Paul Rudolph: If an architect is not an artist, he should not be called an architect. (Interview in Cook and Klotz 1973.)

Gio Ponti: We must always start by considering a work of architecture a work of art and the architect as the artist. (Ponti 1960:71.)

John M. Johansen: The position of the creative architect is a lonely one, for to originate means to have made the creative venture first, and alone. (Interview in Heyer 1966:341.)

Edward Durrell Stone: There is too much conformity in contemporary architecture. I like to think of architecture as an individual creative expression. (Interview in Heyer 1966:177.)

Philip Johnson: Yet we cannot blame everything on our patrons or merely envy Michelangelo, or blame an inartistic business age for not taking us more seriously. . . . What is the answer? Simple—let us build monuments for the masses. . . . People enjoy beautiful automobiles, beautiful and expensive clothes—I am sure they could develop a taste easily enough for beautiful buildings. (Johnson 1973:17, 19.)

If architects had any moral doubts about a retreat from practical and social concerns, structural semiologists provided them with further justification, for they asserted that the value of architecture lies exclusively in its coded meanings (see, for example, Garroni 1980; an attempt to salvage structural semiology from social reactionism is found in Jencks 1981). Further justification for the conception of architecture as pure art comes from aesthetic theorists, including Suzanne Langer (1957:86–89, 1966) and Meyer Schapiro (1978).[2] According to Schapiro (1978), architecture has its comeuppance over the visual arts because architecture (together with music) is pure in that it does not have "to imitate objects but derive[s] effects from elements peculiar to [itself]" (p. 185); yet like painters, architects have the license to "express themselves through forms" (p. 137), and "architects work in abstractions" (p. 228).

Many Are Called But Few Are Chosen

Architects' view of their profession largely relates to the mystique of artistic creativity, and it resonates with the opinions of the top-ranking designers. What is the significance of this extraordinary emphasis on aesthetics—architecture as art—for the human environment, the efficiency and habitability of buildings, towns, and cities? For some time architectural critics and social scientists have expressed concern over these issues (Mumford 1959; Chermayeff and Alexander 1963; Gans 1968; Brett 1971; Goodman 1971; Broady 1973; Mann 1978; Whyte 1968; Friedman 1975). Another problem of interest is the ramifications of this conception for the profession and for practice.

Of the architects interviewed 98 percent mentioned creativity as the distinctive feature of architecture when compared to other professions. To find how architects weigh their own working lives against this ideal, I asked them two additional questions. When they were asked to describe the most important and positive aspect of their work, only 38 percent mentioned anything that related to creativity. When they were asked next what, if anything, they would like to change about their own jobs in their offices, 80 percent answered that they want more opportunities to be creatively engaged ("to have more design assignments"; "have a greater scope of responsibility"; "to be able to work independently in design work").

The problem is that architecture's self-proclaimed mission is successful in that it attracts and trains vast numbers of aspiring artists who define architecture in aesthetic terms. The paradox is that with its exclusive emphasis on individual expression and

in the absence of many opportunities to be designers, most architects are anonymous craftsworkers; yet they lack the dignity
accorded some craftsworkers in earlier times.

Sources of Gratification

In spite of the overwhelming evidence that architects are frus-
trated in terms of what they consider the most important aspect
of their work, there are sources of gratification. Measuring
commitment to job and career is as difficult as measuring how
college students feel about school, the feelings that men and
women have about their spouses, or how patriotic people are.
Each of these is a complex multidimensional psychological phenomenon; besides there is a range of feeling on each dimension, from very negative, to so-so, to very positive. The initial
difficulty is that the dimensions underlying the psychological
phenomenon are not known in advance. The solution is to ask
many questions that conceivably relate to the topic in question,
including some that have been used in past research, and then
try them out with a small number of individuals and modify the
questions before going into the field with the final questionnaire. The intensity, or range of feeling, is built into each item
by using several response categories that range from strongly
agree to strongly disagree. The dimensions are discovered
when the answers are analyzed. Patterns revealed in the analysis
(using factor analysis) indicate which questions tend to go together (that is, the same people tend to agree or disagree with
them) and thus form a cluster. Eighteen questions were asked
that dealt with various facets of commitment, and the analysis of
the answers yielded four different clusters that are separate
dimensions of commitment.[3]

One of these dimensions is based on answers to questions that
reflect contentment with career and a cheerful optimism about
work; it is referred to as Career Contentment. Another is based
on answers to questions that deal with personal recognition
and an interest in the financial rewards of the job; I call this
Professional Egotism. The third dimension is made up of items
that reflect disillusionment with architecture and dissatisfaction
with a variety of features of the job; this is the dimension of
Career Alienation. The final dimension reveals, like the first, a
general satisfaction with work and career but is different from
Career Contentment in that it indicates a greater absorption

with day-to-day work and less of a sense of overall success; an appropriate name for it is Job Satisfaction.

Although a person's position in the firm can make a difference for these forms of commitment, no other personal characteristic—year of degree, type of degree, or reputation of school attended—makes any difference for whether the architect ranks high or low on these dimensions.[4] Also the major characteristics of the firms where the architects work do not affect how architects rank on any of these dimensions either.[5] Hence how content, egotistical, alienated, or satisfied architects are can be explained only by the ways in which their jobs are structured and the opportunities they have had in the firms in which they work.

Career Contentment
In order of their importance in the index, the questions on which Career Contentment is based are the following:

I feel that I can count as friends most of the people with whom I work.

Looking back over the period during which I have been an architect, I feel that I have made very good progress toward my goals.

My work is my most rewarding experience.[6]

Security and confidence, I conclude, are the notable traits of architects who rank high on Career Contentment. The factors that tend to foster high contentment are the following: current responsibility for many different tasks, having had some responsibility on an award-winning project, exercising much power in the firm, and working on many different types of projects.[7] Thus contentment is largely a function of influence, discretion, and opportunities to participate in project design.

Professional Egotism
In order of importance, the questions that comprise this index are the following:

A major source of personal satisfaction for me is recognition by my colleagues.

Financial security was one of my major considerations in choosing architecture as a career.

A major source of personal satisfaction for me is my standing in the community.

In my firm I have a great deal of freedom in doing my own work and in making my own decisions.[8]

Although the emphasis on autonomy, recognition, and financial rewards clearly distinguishes this group of architects who strongly agreed with these questions, what promotes Professional Egotism is similar in two respects to what increases Career Contentment: having the exercise of much power in the firm and having responsibilities for many diverse tasks. Those who rank high on Professional Egotism, quite surprisingly, strongly endorse a design ideology that is humanistic and user oriented and, if you will, antiart.[9] They tend to disagree with such statements as "good design is flair, drama and excitement," and they endorse such statements as "much attention should be given to the users' cultural values, spatial needs, and aesthetic preferences" and "good buildings must relate to their environment."[10]

Career Alienation
In order of importance, the items that make up this index are the following:

If I had more autonomy than I have now I would do a better job as an architect.

I wish I had more responsibility than I have now in my job as an architect.

I identify more closely with my profession, architecture, than with the firm I work in.[11]

The only characteristic that distinguishes architects who score high on the alienation index is a strong identification with the user-oriented ideology, something that they have in common with architects with an egotistical orientation.[12] Such views were not totally heretical in 1974, but lacking full endorsement, architects who held them were treated somewhat suspiciously. The most articulate user-oriented architects called themselves advocacy architects, but facing considerable contempt by their colleagues, they found themselves on the defensive (for an overview of these issues, see Pipkin, La Gory, and Blau 1983; Blau, Pipkin, and La Gory 1983). Although current developments in architectural aesthetics (see Watkin 1977; Tafuri 1980; Scruton 1979; Hubbard 1980) suggest that humanitarian themes may once again be introduced into the frame of the architectural mission, the climate of opinion that prevailed in the 1960s and 1970s was clearly antagonistic to the social significance of architecture. For example, in an interview with Berkeley (1968:87) Hugh Hardy states, "The practice of asking what the community wants is not really helpful to the architects—except politically, or to clarify the program." Johnson (see Heyer 1966:279) remarks, "purpose is not necessary to make a building beautiful . . . sooner or later we will fit our buildings so they can be used . . . where form comes from I don't know, but it has nothing at all to do with the functional or sociological aspects of our architecture." To set the record straight where architecture stood with respect to occupations with practical and social concerns, Johnson (1973:19) states that "in spite of the theories of the . . . para-architectural occupations . . . social planning, landscaping, ecology studies, and regional planning . . . we have an art of architecture still."

Given such sentiments of the leaders of the profession, it is no wonder that architects who felt that "much more attention should be given to the users' cultural values, spatial needs, and aesthetic preferences" express alienation and estrangement from their work.

Job Satisfaction

The three items in order of importance that make up the scale of job satisfaction are the following:

I have enough authority to do my job well.

My work is my most rewarding experience.

I am very satisfied when I compare my present job with similar jobs in other firms.[13]

Architects who are highly satisfied with their work have many diverse responsibilities and have more power than most others.[14] Hardly different in detail from the findings for the other forms of commitment, notably Career Contentment, these results help to confirm through replication that the two major sources of commitment are voice and diversity of responsibilities. The opposite is also true: lack of satisfaction and low career contentment are largely due to having narrowly specialized responsibilities and the failure to exercise much voice in professional decisions.

Summary

The results for commitment can be summarized:

• *Career Contentment:* Many tasks, worked on award-winning projects, power, many types of projects.

• *Professional Egotism:* Power, humanitarian orientation, many tasks.

• *Career Alienation:* Humanitarian orientation.

• *Job Satisfaction:* Many tasks, power, many types of projects.

To be emphasized is that the chief source of low commitment is the discrepancy between what architects believe defines the profession—creative design—and what in fact they find themselves engaged in. Because there are few opportunities—there are many more jobs in production than in design and more commonplace buildings than chefs d'oeuvre—this is practically a universal problem among architects. Yet underlying this pervasive pattern is variation with respect to the degree to which architects are generalists or specialists and also with respect to how much influence they have.

Diverse tasks as well as voice are salient for commitment, and we know from chapter 2 that the relative size of the firm is important for being a generalist or specialist (see figure 2.1). In small offices, compared with large ones, architects are more likely to be generalists, which is a source of power in the affairs of their firms. This is generally true but not invariably; small firms also offer fewer services than large ones, which reduces the likelihood that architects are generalists, and this partially reduces the power they otherwise have. It is likely that variation in the internal organization of offices will help to clarify why some offices have more generalists and others more specialists. Interviews with staff members from the American Institute of Architects (AIA), with firm heads, and with architects indicated that there are two prototypical structures: one is vertical, based on project teams, and the other is horizontal, based on departments. In vertical offices a project is assigned to one subunit and more or less remains in that subunit through completion. In the departmentalized office the project moves from one unit to another—from project analysis, to design, to detailed drawings, specifications, estimation, and so forth. In the first, architects do more or less everything; in the second, architects must be specialists; and typically in very small offices, the entire office comprises a project team. Figure 3.1 illustrates contrasting structures for the large firm.

Implications of Organizational Differences

The distinction between a structure of function-based departments and that of project teams derives from traditional theories for industrial management (Gulick and Urwick 1937). Organization by departments involves a process in which a product—say, a mass-produced car—moves horizontally through different operations and different departments. Organization by semiautonomous units is one in which a product—say, a custom-made racing car—is under the jurisdiction of a team of expert designers and mechanics. Quite naturally the former type of organization has been considered superior in industry because top management can exercise greater control and because of the efficiencies that relate to economies of specialization.

As architecture firms become very large, coordination problems create pressures to departmentalize, although there are exceptions, such as the office of I. M. Pei (see Blake 1973). Firms with fewer than around fifty or sixty architects show greater variation compared with smaller and larger offices in their organization. Lacking systematic data on the form of offices, the interviews I had with architects provide evidence for why organization by project teams is probably responsible for the connections I find between engaging in diverse tasks and commitment.[15]

A senior architect of a Manhattan office described her firm as one set up vertically into project teams. First citing the disadvantages of the vertical structure, she said, "Sometimes it's not efficient—when designers get involved in drafting work," but added, "the advantage is that you can hire people who want to be architects in the best sense. You may not get the best experts, and things go wrong, but then you do get an integrated design concept with the same people working on it, and the project is handled more responsibly." A partner of another firm organized by project teams observed, "The advantage is that every aspect of design and production is considered important because there is a core idea for the project to which everyone closely relates." This architect recounts his experiences as an

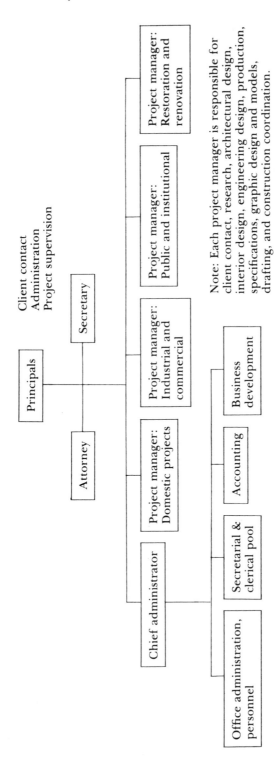

Principals
Client contact
Administration
Project supervision

Attorney

Secretary

Chief administrator

Project manager:
Domestic projects

Project manager:
Industrial and
commercial

Project manager:
Public and institutional

Project manager:
Restoration and
renovation

Office administration,
personnel

Secretarial &
clerical pool

Accounting

Business
development

Note: Each project manager is responsible for
client contact, research, architectural design,
interior design, engineering design, production,
specifications, graphic design and models,
drafting, and construction coordination.

A. Organization by Project Team

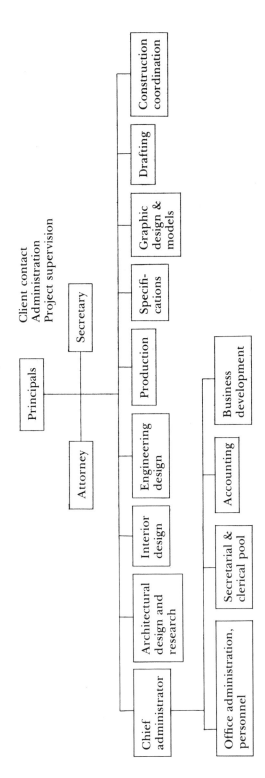

B. Organization by Department

Figure 3.1
Contrasting structures for large office

employee in the Japanese firm of Fumihiko Maki in response to my query about the differences between the two types of firms:

Even though one person was not totally responsible for a building, he felt his responsibility was as great as Maki's was, and his commitment was total. Decisions were made in a very democratic way, with no person's suggestions eliminated until all could see the natural course a particular design would take. It was quite an exhilarating experience. In the best offices, Le Corbusier's office, for example, each employee would be in charge of a single job and carry it through from start to finish . . . the pure form of your vertically organized office. Corbusier would act as a sort of critic, floating from one to another. He would only spend half the day in the office and the rest painting. . . . I can't think of any office anywhere of any quality that isn't set up vertically. The esprit de corps is greater certainly than having to be part of some production line. There is nothing that kills creativity more than the isolation of people into job functions.

Based on the experiences of architects, it appears that the vertical subdivision of offices into teams, each handling a project from start to finish, is superior in terms of architects' commitment. The reason is that team organization gives architects opportunities to be generalists and to have diverse responsibilities. It also gives them greater voice in decisions.

Conclusions

In many fields in which creativity is a prime value and source of reward, there is a proliferation of roles that are equally legitimate. In the scholarly community Znaniecki (1940) distinguishes a number of them: the discoverer of truth, the eclectic, the historian, the disseminator, the discoverer of facts, the discoverer of problems. In architecture the prime value of creativity has become increasingly exclusive, defined in the narrow terms of design. More than that it has become the master value as architecture is increasingly defined as important only insofar as it is art.

Art excluded, architecture is in disassembly. Urban design concepts have been paid little heed (Barnett 1974), innovative engineering technology is far beyond the boundaries of an aesthetically based architecture (Banham 1980:329–330; Frampton 1980), and little recognition is paid to interior design or to restoration (interview with Polshek in Diamonstein 1980:196–197). And social planning, landscaping, ecology studies, and regional studies are considered paraarchitectural (Johnson 1973). The absence in architecture of many equally valued roles helps to explain why there is such a discrepancy between what architects expect from their careers and what they experience. These conclusions are supported by Salaman's (1974) study of British architects as well; he finds the main source of disappointment to be the lack of opportunity to use skills and knowledge acquired in training and especially the lack of opportunities to participate in design.

After analytically excising the major frustration—the lack of opportunities to create and design—the residual gratification in architecture is found to derive from the opportunities to exercise voice—to have power to influence decisions—and to have wide and diverse responsibilities. The persistent linkage of these two factors makes them especially important for defining the nature of professionalism in architecture. Although there is considerable variation from one office to another in terms of architects' benefiting from these opportunities, the office that is subdivided into smaller self-contained components is the one that is structurally more conducive to providing such opportunities.

Perhaps the emphasis on high art is a contemporary fashion, which will eventually pass. In the meantime there are concerns—social, environmental, political, and economic—about the accumulation of both shabbiness and swank. Architecture lasts a while, yet mediocre buildings long outlive their functions, and pretentious buildings are not so easily deacquisitioned as the high art they emulate. Yet this study addresses not these issues so much as the consequences of the singular emphasis on art for the profession and practice of architecture.

The conclusions that I have reached are that owing to the singular master value of design creativity, most architects are destined to fail to realize their aspirations and they know that. The contradictions that ensue when a master value is not accompanied by wide-ranging opportunities to work in terms of that value are bound to create the conditions for great disillusionment (or apostacy) and the eventual inability of the profession to attract new recruits who possess talent and exciting ideas. The failure of the profession to imbue other work—restoration, urban design, advocacy architecture, interiors—with dignity and esteem serves to heighten these contradictions. An entire profession can founder under such circumstances; tenacious and confounded contradictions are self-reinforcing. These conclusions, based on the evidence of a social survey, are consistent with those of Andrew Saint, an architectural critic. He writes (1983:164), "Analogy with the pure arts, therefore, has perverted the proper meaning of imagination in architecture. . . . If architects wish to preserve the better elements in professionalism and to prevent their calling from degenerating, except in a few instances, to a mere trade, they must find a way to break the barriers limiting the concept of imagination to art and design."

Imagination will and ought never disappear from architecture. Buildings will always be given personalities, and architects will always have convictions about style, the topic I next address.

4

Convictions and Agendas

Slow radicals is Arnold Foster's (1976) characterization of visual artists because the convictions of artists surpass the tastes of the public and only gradually change opinions and affect social change. This chapter identifies the nature of the dilemmas that make rank-and-file architects slow radicals but shows that they are so in a way that is very different from the painter's alienation from the public, as described by Foster and others (see Shapiro 1976; Taylor 1961; Shawn 1957; Rosenberg 1964; Schapiro 1978).

In the first instance, the question is whether artists act on their own convictions, regardless of public standards and taste. To return to myths, convictions lead artists to incur great risks that often result in grave consequences. Not only did Icarus fall from the sky, but Daedalus, one legend tells us, killed his pupil Talus over rivalry about which was considered the better artist; Pandora was created by the artist Haphaetros; Pygmalion's statue, at least in one version of the legend, came to life as Aphrodite, who instigated the Trojan war; and the heroized architect in sundry Jewish, Christian, Swedish, and German legends is variously transformed into ape, devil, or pagan giant. Modern literary themes also echo the message of romantic heroism and the tragic consequences of creative genius.[1]

Contemporary architects embrace progressive, even radical, ideas, but because these ideas are under various constraints and are therefore risky to act on, they are slow to be realized. Firm heads, in contrast, have notions about their offices that are right in step with the times. They can be described as fast pragmatists. The first topic to be considered is architects' convictions—their deeply held beliefs about how buildings ought to look and to function—and the second is the agendas of firm heads—the goals and objectives principals set for the work carried out in their offices.

Specificity Premise

I have already discussed how situational alienation, evident in specialization and powerlessness in organizations, is the source of low commitment among architects. This parallels findings reported for many other types of artists. For example, main sources of frustration for painters include dependence on commercial markets, bureaucratic constraints imposed by the institutions with which they are connected and the rationalization of art collection practices (Pelles 1963; Rosenberg and Fliegel 1965; Adler 1979). Comparable problems are experienced by symphony musicians (Rosenberg and Rosenberg 1979; Faulkner 1973; Westby 1960), opera performers (Martorella 1982), composers (Nash 1955), and filmmakers (Faulkner 1983). In all but their details, these conclusions have been anticipated by socialist scholars, including Ernst Fischer (1959), Herbert Read (1966), and William Morris.

Yet it is striking that with the exception of architecture, artistic innovation proceeds at an astonishing rate in contemporary capitalistic societies, in spite of pervasive bureaucratization, materialistic values, the paucity of economic subsidies, and competition from mass-produced and commercial arts. Aesthetic theorists explain that art is independent of exigencies of its context generally and of the political economy of capitalism in particular. This is termed the premise of specificity of art. Although there is some disagreement about just how autonomous, or isolated, art is from its historical and social situation, Wolff (1983) summarizes the main argument:

emphasis on specificity takes up the . . . question of the independence of art in relation to social or economic factors. Here the concepts of "specificity" and "relative autonomy" are more or less interchangeable. This line of argument . . . maintains that although art is a social product (which is, however, thanks to the historical separation of the aesthetic as a distinct sphere, regarded and experienced as remote from its social determinants) it is also the case that it is not simply a reflection of its social origins. . . . *The relative autonomy of art and culture consists in the specific codes and conventions of artistic representation, which mediate and (re)produce ideology in aesthetic form.* (P. 80; emphasis added.)

Wolff thus suggests that art products are autonomous because of the primary autonomy of artistic ideologies. An alternative formulation, which would better explain historical developments in architecture, is that products themselves are subject to historical, social, and economic constraints, but aesthetic convictions are not, and may even exist in opposition to these constraints. This interpretation has some support in the writings of Marxist scholars, including Vázquez (1973), Marcuse (1978), and Morawski (1974). As Vázquez (1973:101) states, "Art is an autonomous sphere, but its autonomy exists only *by, in,* and *through* its social conditioning. . . . However, the internal [immanent] logic of artistic development tends to affirm the relative autonomy of art; this autonomy in turn explains why there is no exact correspondence between the internal and the external, that is, between socio-historical and artistic development.

In examining the convictions of architects, the fundamental questions center on how these convictions correspond with what is actually built and how both convictions and built architecture are related to the sociohistorical conditions in which they develop. I do not deal with all of these questions at once; some of the answers depend partly on material presented in subsequent chapters. What I consider here is the degree to which architects' convictions are in agreement or conflict with the agendas set by the heads of firms and the degree to which both convictions and agendas are consistent with the prevailing character of built architecture. My initial assumption is that the premise of specificity means, in architecture at least, that convictions exhibit autonomy from sociohistorical conditions but products do not.

Convictions of Architects

In general architects have deeply felt beliefs about buildings: their function, what meanings they express, their style, the ideas they impart, and their rhetorical or audience effects.[2] Thus convictions are a many-faceted mix of the cognitive and the normative. This is not to say that they are haphazard; they are, for various reasons, very well structured, albeit identifying that

structure is not always easy.[3] Convictions serve practitioners—artists and architects—in essentially the same manner that
theories serve critics and the public. Without theories there
would be, according to Danto (1964), no art world, no art. To
make the point for theory (one that holds also for convictions)
Danto (1981) states:

I proposed that we cannot perceive the aesthetic qualities of
artworks, as distinct from the aesthetic qualities of their material
counterparts, until the concept of art is available to us. But I
have now taken this point a step further. There is a whole range
of predicates beyond the standard aesthetic predicates which
have application to artworks and not to real things, nor, for
that matter to the material counterparts of the artworks. For it
would be strange to speak of flowers as powerful, it would be
equally strange to speak of scribbled and splotched paper as
powerful. (P. 158.)

Art, in short, is sustained by concepts and interpretation. An
important difference not to be missed is that theories about art
most often take into account the relativity of aesthetic criteria
with respect to time and place (see Schapiro 1953; Gombrich
1951), whereas convictions are held by practitioners with certitude. As Becker (1974:773) observes, artists do not consider
that their conventions are merely "arbitrary and conventional;
they feel that they are natural, proper, and normal."

Throughout history in the arts, styles changed very slowly,
and at any given time convictional hegemony tended to prevail.
This pattern was broken, at least for the visual arts, when a
surplus of trained artists in nineteenth-century France created
opportunities for new markets, which in turn stimulated innovation (White and White 1965; Rogers 1970). But in architecture this failed to occur. Instead the style of Beaux Arts was
simply replaced by that of another, the international style, which
around the mid-1970s only barely appeared to give way to
(convictional) pluralism.

Three exhibits mark the beginning of change or, at the very
least, according to Goldberger (1976a), some quarreling among
architects about the possibility of change. One was a retrospective, "The Architecture of the Ecole des Beaux Arts," held at
the Museum of Modern Art in New York City in 1975, a second
was the 1976 Chicago Museum of Contemporary Art exhibit
that celebrated the international style, and the third, "The

Chicago Architects Show," a salon des refusés, staged in Chicago in protest of the Museum of Contemporary Art show that represented a more romantic, eclectic alternative to modernism. Critics were uniform in their pronouncements that these exhibits augured something of importance, but no one could say exactly what. Goldberger (1975:38) interpreted the New York show as a "synthesis of pragmatism and symbolism," though he hedged to term it an endorsement of new principles of postmodernism of whatever variety. Huxtable (1975) treated the New York show more as an admonishment of the impoverishment of the international style but after the Chicago shows, she (1976) was clearer in her assessment of the changes: "History and hedonism are back." Contrasting the theme of the exhibit at the Chicago Museum of Contemporary Art with that of the confrontational show, Davis (1976) notes that the latter reveals that the "younger generation of architects is fed up with logic and consistency."

In short it was impossible to know, on the basis of critics' pronouncements, in which specific direction(s) architecture would be pointed. Art deco, Venturi's theory of "complexity and contradiction," Venturi's pop style of built architecture, adhocism, Cheapskate architecture, a Beaux Arts revival, the classy style of Moore: all were possibilities as even was, Huxtable (1975) mentioned, a more humane architecture.

Architects in this study were asked about their aesthetic convictions in 1974, one year before the influential Beaux Arts show and two years before the establishment and antiestablishment shows in Chicago. This was a year in which most observers would have predicted that rank-and-file architects would still endorse, if only halfheartedly, the international style. One could even infer this from the buildings most firms were designing at the time.

Architects were asked two sets of questions to discover their convictions about architecture. Because architects are notoriously unwilling or unable to talk about their own design approaches (Salaman 1974:98), the questions were designed to be impersonal and indirect yet comprehensive and attractive to architects. By the standards of survey research, they are somewhat unconventional. I asked first about their architectural heroes and rascals. Then I provided them with a list of quotations (most of which are well known in the architectural community and serve various schools as aphorisms or as counteraphorisms) and asked how much they agreed or disagreed with each one.

Heroes and Rascals
On the questionnaire fifty names (of individual architects, teams, groups, and some architectural critics) were listed in alphabetical order. Respondents were asked, "For those that you know, indicate whether you generally tend to like or dislike their work or contributions. There will probably be some on the list that you do not know; please indicate this with a check in the last column." Obviously not all important architects and critics could be included; the objective, however, was to include to the extent possible the full range of design approaches, controversies, and theories in evidence during the mid-1970s. As one base for comparison, several eminent, deceased individuals

Table 4.1
Evaluations of works of heroes and rascals

Name	% "like" (1)	% "know" (2)	Ratio of "like" to "know" (3)
1. Le Corbusier	95	100	0.95
2. Louis Kahn	95	99	.95
3. Frank Lloyd Wright	93	99	.94
4. Eero Saarinen	92	99	.93
5. Alvar Aalto	91	93	.97
6. Pier Luigi Nervi	91	97	.93
7. Mies van der Rohe	83	96	.87
8. Walter Gropius	82	97	.84
9. I. M. Pei	82	99	.83
10. Marcel Breuer	78	98	.79
11. Richard Neutra	78	94	.83
12. The Architects' Collaborative	78	90	.86
13. Kenzo Tange	78	86	.91
14. Charles & Ray Eames	76	83	.91
15. Buckminster Fuller	72	92	.79
16. Paul Rudolph	72	99	.73
17. José Sert	67	82	.81
18. Oscar Niemeyer	67	95	.70
19. Moshe Safdie	66	87	.76
20. The Cambridge 7	65	74	.87
21. Edward Larrabee Barnes	65	86	.76
22. Philip Johnson	62	96	.65
23. Romaldo Giurgola	61	73	.83
24. John M. Johansen	60	83	.73
25. Richard Meier	60	80	.75

(such as Mies van der Rohe) were included, as were various vanguard architects or groups (such as Archigram), and, to set another baseline, Albert Speer, director of building in Berlin under Hitler.

The names are ordered in table 4.1 by the percentage of the architects who like their work. Without describing in detail the patterns that can be discovered in this rank order, a few general observations might be made. Nine of the top ten heroes are deceased, which in all likelihood is a reflection of the importance of tradition for the way that architects view and solve design problems. This is not surprising; even when tradition is most fervently being attacked, the masters of that tradition are prominent as they provide the foil for new alternatives (see Huxtable 1983). Some of the eminent individuals are critics who have taken architects to task for their insensitivity to the social

Table 4.1 (continued)

Name	% "like" (1)	% "know" (2)	Ratio of "like" to "know" (3)
26. Charles Moore	56	72	.78
27. Skidmore, Owings, & Merrill	55	96	.57
28. Hugh Stubbins	51	76	.67
29. Paolo Soleri	50	86	.58
30. James Stirling	49	54	.92
31. Jane Jacobs	46	68	.68
32. Victor Lundy	44	72	.62
33. Minoru Yamasaki	44	98	.45
34. Robert Venturi	42	86	.49
35. Herb Greene	39	49	.78
36. Bruce Goff	38	66	.57
37. Percival & Paul Goodman	36	61	.59
38. Gerhard Kallman	33	43	.75
39. Aldo van Eyck	32	36	.88
40. Matthew Nowicki	28	36	.78
41. Archigram	27	44	.61
42. Ezra Ehrenkrantz	26	37	.70
43. Frederick Kiesler	25	40	.63
44. Joseph Esherick	23	29	.77
45. Wallace Harrison	20	87	.23
46. Edward Durrell Stone	19	98	.20
47. Konrad Wachsmann	18	27	.66
48. Morris Lapidus	17	88	.20
49. Superstudio	7	15	.49
50. Albert Speer	4	47	.09

integrity of neighborhoods and the needs of communities and cities. Such critics, notably Jane Jacobs and Percival and Paul Goodman, are not viewed as negatively by these architects as one might expect. Many of the lowest ranking are architects who have decisively challenged the assumptions that underlie mainstream design. These include three individual designers— Kiesler, Esherick, and Wachsmann—and the Florence-based group, Superstudio. Kiesler's unconventional and even radical departures from the work of his contemporaries in the 1920s are considered to be too precocious and premature to have had a direct impact on the work of most contemporary architects, although Frampton (1980:243) mentions they probably influenced Kahn's work. These projects of the 1920s were based on the conception of continuous curves, egg-shaped, and void of any planes, a conception that nonetheless is evident in his more recent and best-known project (with Armand Bartos), Jerusalem's Shrine of the Book, the museum for the Dead Sea Scrolls.

The percentage of architects who know the work of the fifty is reported in column 2. The ratio is given in column 3 of the number of times they were mentioned favorably by the respondents to the number of times their work was reported as being known.

A comparison of columns 2 and 3 can identify a number of architects who are not generally known but who are well liked by a few followers (the value in column 2 is relatively low and that in column 3 high). Each of these provides either an indication of a small but possibly growing school in architecture or the persistence of a dedicated following. One individual who meets this criterion is Greene, a midwestern architect who was among the first American architects to react against the minimalist traditions of the international style; he established his reputation with a decompositional approach to design and the incorporation into buildings of incongruous materials—shingles, steel, brick, glass, and other elements specific to the site of the building. C. Ray Smith (1977:68–69) describes his expressive house designs (along with the work of Kiesler and Goff) as part of a witty and whimsical revolution against the simple rectilinear box. He calls it "free-for-all architecture," while Tafuri (1980: 126, 138) describes it as revisionist and as anticipating a new dada.

Esherick is also someone not generally known among Manhattan architects, but he is highly regarded by those who know his work. Although Esherick's projects have been characterized as Kahnian because of the emphasis on strong forms and intersecting spaces, his projects on the whole exhibit more eclectic sources than that of a single school. Dominant overhanging screens in his California houses of the early 1960s met functional requirements, according to Esherick (interview in Heyer 1966:112), but these were transformed to meet more explicit design objectives in the mid-1960s. The Environmental Design Building at the University of California's Berkeley campus has obvious connections with traditions of brutalismo in that the materials themselves become frank design elements. Esherick's 1968 Cannery is yet another departure from his previous work. A reconverted DelMonte canning plant located near San Francisco's Ghirardelli Square is more Esheresque than brutalismo, more pop than Kahnian. Moore (1968:76–79) describes it as an irrational maze with pedestrian turns in a zigzag pattern and brickwork that surpasses anything Byzantine.

Another architect who has a small and dedicated following is Matthew Nowicki. It is not surprising that he is not well known; he died in a plane crash at the age of forty one, and most of his projects (including his design for Chandigarh, plans for which were later completed by Le Corbusier) were not built. Nowicki, however, along with Buckminster Fuller, established a series of proposals to link a conception of humanistic ideals with advanced technology, and because of his engineering training in Warsaw contributed to the development of prefabrication, the mushroom column, and modular building. Mumford (1954: 175) describes Nowicki as "one of the most creative architects of his generation."

Two others are included in this group: Stirling (considered later) and van Eyck. The reason, I suspect, that Aldo van Eyck is not better known in New York is that most of his completed projects are located in the Netherlands, with a few in other European countries and Lima, and none in North America. His buildings are intricate and complex, which stems from his insistence that inhabitants have alternatives and choices that are not predetermined in advance. At the same time, as evident particularly in the Children's Home in Amsterdam, the spaces are intimate and self-contained, conducive to bonds of community and family. Although the focus of most scholarly reviews of his projects is his fundamental humanity, attention increasingly centers on the timelessness of his aesthetic conceptions, the way in which he fuses elements of the past and present, and how he anticipates the future (Curtis 1983:385).

Contrasted with this group who have achieved high renown among a few is a group of antiheroes: architects neither widely known nor appreciated by those who do know them (the values in columns 2 and 3 are relatively low). Speer, not unexpectedly, is unappreciated, as are, for different reasons, two avant-garde movements—Archigram and Superstudio—and Karl Wachsmann.

Finally, an interesting group are those architects who are well known and controversial (the values in columns 2 and 3 are, respectively, high and low): Lapidus, Venturi, Skidmore, Owings & Merrill (SOM), Yamasaki, Harrison, and Stone. The independence of Lapidus, whose garish Miami Beach hotel shocked AIA conventioneers, and also of Venturi (the champion of complexity and ambiguity yet the designer of the poultry stand that looks like a duck and of a gold-colored television antenna that is not intended to work) has made them centers of controversy.[4] But it is indeed surprising that SOM, Yamasaki, Harrison, and Stone are also controversial, for they are major representatives of the international style, which was still the major influence in building in the 1970s.

Although these results indicate some muddle in the prevailing ideas and beliefs of architects, an identification of an underlying structure indicates a clarity and explains why, for example, the work of Archigram appears to be associated with that of Speer but is in fact only spuriously so.

Underlying Structure

It is important to emphasize that the summary responses of rank-and-file architects in table 4.1 simply describe how well they generally like or dislike the work of prominent individuals and groups in the field and how well they know their work. How the responding architects perceive the various styles represented by them as connected is a more important problem, since from connections can be inferred criteria for defining schools of thought or clusters of design styles. Factor analysis is used for this purpose—to identify schools or design clusters and to isolate the underlying dimensions that account for them. It is assumed that when large numbers of responding individuals like (or dislike) the work of the same architects, these architects constitute a distinct grouping, and their design approaches or their theories have a basic similarity. The dimensions that account for these clusters reveal a theoretical structure that extends beyond a description of the responses (Boudon 1971: 52–89, 133). Moreover that theoretical structure clarifies many more connections than critical analysis can possibly do because of the extraordinarily large numbers of comparisons being made. (Specifically there are 1,225 paired comparisons.)

The interpretation of each factor (and the label it is given) is based on the relative magnitudes of the factor loadings. They measure which variables are involved in defining a factor and to what degree the variables are important. Whereas a given factor loading indicates the relative importance of a particular variable, the importance of a given factor is indicated by the amount of the variation in all of the answers for which it can account.

Because of the large number of the questions asked, the dimensions that result from the factor analyses presented here are assumed to be relatively stable. In other words, had I asked about other specific eminent individuals and groups of the same architects or asked the same questions of different Manhattan architects, it is likely that similar or identical dimensions would have emerged.

Although fourteen factors were generated, four describe most of the variation in these data and thus explain by and large the underlying structure.[5] The four factors are defined here in terms of the names of architects and groups and are listed from most to least important (that is, in terms of the amount of variation in the answers for which they can account):[6]

Factor I: Subjectivism versus formalism

Stirling	.58
Aalto	.46
Yamasaki	−.66
Stone	−.66
Harrison	−.63
Speer	−.44
Lapidus	−.44

Factor II: Purist

Neutra	.56
Niemeyer	.55
Nervi	.42

Factor III: Meta-art

Wachsmann	.49
Archigram	.45
Superstudio	.43

Factor IV: Camp

Meier	.55
Rudolph	.44

The most popular architects—for example, Le Corbusier, Kahn, Wright, and Saarinen in table 4.1—do not appear in the first four factors, nor do they have high loadings on any of the fourteen factors that make up the complete solution. The reason is that they do not have a distinctive group of followers; because they are so generally popular, opinions about them tend not to vary greatly and so do not explain the differences in opinions about architects and styles. In general, the higher the factor loading, the more distinctive the group of admirers.

Antithetical meanings (indicated by the contrast of positive and negative factor loadings) are revealed by the first factor. I interpret this as the opposition between subjectivism and formalism. Because this factor accounts for more of the variance than any other (about twice as much), it can be inferred that it reveals most about the currents of thought in contemporary architecture. Furthermore, significance can be attached to its bipolarity, for it indicates underlying disagreements as to the assumptions that architects bring to their understanding of the field and to their own work. Specifically, the results show that architects who like the qualities evident in the work of Aalto and Stirling tend to dislike those in the work of Stone, Yamasaki, Harrison, Lapidus, and Speer, and vice-versa. Although the latter pattern is rarer—the second set of architects are less popular than the first—the opposition highlights an underlying major value conflict in architecture.

What do members of each of the two sets share? Let us consider first the set with the positive factor loadings: Stirling and Aalto. Ostensibly they have little in common. Stirling is English, and having started his career in the mid-1950s under the banner of brutalismo became best known for his glass buildings, particularly the history faculty building at Cambridge University. In contrast Aalto, a Finn, began practice in the 1920s. Although early in his career he was influenced by both functionalism and Soviet constructivism, his later works show little of these two styles. Aside from these differences, each has expressed strong concerns with the common folk, indicated in Stirling's projects for Latin American *barriadas* and in Aalto's buildings that are preeminently scaled and designed to meet human needs. To capture similarities in style and expression, Jencks's (1971, 1973) classification scheme, the "evolutionary tree," as well as Frampton's (1980) and Joedicke's (1969) historical comparisons, are useful.

Jencks is nothing less than enthusiastic about the "powerful rhetoric" of James Stirling (1973:261): "For the first time since the Palm House at Kew or the Crystal Palace, Britain had a designer who could handle glass with virility; for the first time since MacKintosh, an architect who could combine glass with a moulded masonry on top of itself, one masterful conceit following another into the clouds." Frampton (1980:268) describes Stirling's university series in similar terms: "the brilliant architectonic of [Stirling's] form, . . . with its tendency to dismember and recombine discrete architectural elements, partly in response to empirical demands and partly out of a determination to 'deconstruct' the received forms of the Modern Movement."

Jencks (1973:28, 31, 44–45) classifies Stirling in the "metaphysical idealist" tradition because of his "expressive functionalism" and "alternatives to the existing social system." For him the contrast between Stirling's and Aalto's work is formal and not "necessarily semantic" for they share the belief that architecture must help realize a set of social ideals that are defined, however vaguely, in terms of "liberalism and equality." Unlike Stirling's complexity, Aalto's style is more organic. Jencks (1973:179–183) describes Aalto's interiors as "undulating surfaces" and "interrelated shapes," and, taken as a whole, his buildings as "relaxed," often looking like "crouching animals." Yet in his classification scheme, Jencks (1973:167–184) places Aalto close to Stirling in the "heroic idealist" tradition because of the plasticity and expressiveness of form. Frampton (1980:197–202, 268) states that a main commonality is ambiguity of space, although Stirling's more recent projects, he suggests, have less ambience and "place" attributes, which are enduring qualities throughout all of Aalto's work. Joedicke

(1969:108–137) considers Aalto and Stirling to be at different points in the same tradition; Aalto is the forerunner and Stirling a high point of "international brutalism," which is characterized by the breakdown of functional units, complexity, individuality, and, more generally, subjectivity.

Such common features of the projects of Aalto and Stirling suggest that this pole be termed *subjectivism,* and this becomes even more evident when they are compared with architects in the opposite set.

Speer's fascist colossi and American modern architecture are generally not linked together, although a few architectural critics have seen the underlying similarity, which the statistical procedure, factor analysis, makes apparent. With little sympathy, Jencks (1973:28, 185, 200) discusses Stone, Yamasaki, and Harrison as direct descendants of Speer—their projects are "self-conscious" and "bureaucratic." When Hughes (1981:108) refers to the work of the partnership of Harrison and Abromovitz, he frankly states, "The scariest example we have of [the architecture of state power] is the seat of government for New York State, Albany Mall. . . . This place makes Albert Speer's projects seem delicate." Tom Wolfe (1981:92) describes Stone's Kennedy Center, with its six-story lobby and length of six hundred and thirty feet, as "playing up to American megalomania." Only in the social implications of their works is Joedicke (1969:67) more charitable; he describes the buildings of these three—Stone, Yamasaki, Harrison—as formalistic—that is, as stressing form over content, as being monumental and artificial.

Speer is unappreciated by the vast majority of these architects yet appears on the same pole of the first dimension because these Manhattan architects associate his work with buildings by Yamasaki, Stone, Harrison, and Lapidus. Although Hitler failed to see the connection between the Bauhaus and Reich-approved architecture, the fact that Speer is joined with a descendant style of the Bauhaus on a dimension of architects' convictions provides a parody on the international style—a joke, too, on history.

Lapidus's work is distinctly different from the others in this cluster, but he is grouped with them as discerned in the patterns in architects' responses, which indicates that architects perceive underlying similarities in style or conception. Ada Louise Huxtable, it is reported by Smith (1977:214), called Lapidus's Miami Beach hotels "high kitsch" and "uninspired super-schlock."

Although Lapidus stresses how much "fun" it is, the Fountaine-bleau by anyone's standards is also garish, monumental, super-ornate. It is ventured here that serious monuments for the state or corporate enterprises and frivolous ones for the leisure of the rich serve the same ultimate values, values that under-lie bureaucratic power, concentrated wealth, and corporate elitism.

Thus, factor I contrasts the subjective and expressive with the formal and contrived. There was little (built) evidence in 1974 that American architecture was on the threshold of a humanistic transformation (nor is there much now), but these results indi-cate that any future change, to be consistent with architects' beliefs, would be toward the humanistic standards of Aalto and Stirling rather than the standards of the monumental and im-personal or those of the garish and chic represented by the contrasting traditions.

Factor II, which I call the purist dimension, includes Neutra, best known for his West Coast houses made of steel and so much glass that they are "distinctly nonprivate" (see Drexler and Hines 1982), and Niemeyer, one of the major figures of the Brasilia scheme. Jencks (1973:28) places both in the "idealistic international style" tradition. Nervi is also included in this fac-tor. He is the most popular of the three (liked by 91 percent of the respondents), and the relatively low factor loading of 0.42 indicates that he has a less distinctive following than either Neutra or Niemeyer. Nervi, an Italian engineer, is labeled by Jencks (1973:28) as an example of "logical functionalism." His works, according to Jencks, are distinct from the "idealistic in-ternational style," represented by the buildings of Neutra and Niemeyer, insofar as Nervi uses the inherent logic of structural materials to exploit their expressive potentiality, rather than their formal purity.

But if style is not what Neutra and Niemeyer have in common with Nervi, why are they implicitly associated by the architects in the sample? While Aalto and Stirling's buildings have been praised for their intimate spaces and congeniality, Neutra, Niemeyer, and Nervi have exhibited a marked disregard, in-deed often a contempt, for people and their needs. Niemeyer's Brasilia, with its zoned segregation by social class and general absence of amenities, is unlivable for poor and rich alike (Bill 1954). Neutra's work "has always had an unreal absolute look to it, as if it had just been extruded from some Platonic kitchen where dirt and age had been externally expunged" (Jencks 1973:215). And Nervi's engineering masterpieces are awesome megasculptures, with their vast columnless spaces spanned by parabolic forms. Such monuments overwhelm but do not invite. It is this quality of uninhabitability that Nervi's buildings share with the architecture of Neutra and Niemeyer despite ostensible differences in style.

Wachsmann, Archigram, and Superstudio are grouped together in factor III, which indicates that despite their obvious differences they are linked with one another by working architects. Political, technological, and societal objectives figure in the explicit intentions of Wachsmann, Archigram, and Superstudio although in different mixtures and with different emphases. A unitary theme they share is that architecture must be redefined in nonartistic terms—that is, as an activity that transcends art.

The meta-art notion is evident in Wachsmann's technocratic projects (for example, in his space frames and modular systems) and in his writings. Among his theses for an industrialized building program, he (1975:156) states, "The machine is the tool of our age. It is the cause of those effects through which the social order manifests itself." In contrast to Wachsmann's orientation to change through technocratic means, Archigram and Superstudio can be considered political and literary movements that involve architecture in a somewhat fantastical way. Founded in 1961 Archigram was tied in part to technocratic ideologies and then moved to space-age projects and to designs for plug-in megastructures. To illustrate, one manifesto states (Banham and Price 1960), "What we want, clearly, is a miniaturized, mobile, cooking, refrigerating, sewage-disposing, VHF and three-channel-televiewing, trunk-dialing, dry-cleaning and martini-dispensing services robot with fitted ash-trays and book rest, that will follow us around the house riding on a cushion of air like an interplanetary hoover."

Members of Superstudio describe themselves as utopian revolutionaries. Early writings by the Situationists, one faction of Superstudio, advocated the "free and equal association of producers" (Situationists 1960). Projects include "The Continuous Monument," a unitary town that extends around the world and in which everyone has an identical room, and "A Journey from A to B," which eliminates roads, architecture, as well as any semblance of a built environment, technology, and consumer goods. Superstudio does not go unnoticed by the critics. Frampton (1980:286) writes, "in short, the quintessential anti-architectural utopia." And Jencks (1973:56) asks, "Is it fascism or democracy?" The answer is, it is the avant-garde, which at all times swims in political currents but often without clearly discernable direction.

The last factor includes two fairly well-known New York architects: Paul Rudolph, whose exuberant Art and Architecture Building at Yale University created so much controversy, and Richard Meier, a member of the school variously called the "cardboard corbu," the "Whites," the "New York School," and "The Five." His buildings, Rudolph claims, are "to excite and to challenge," and he accepts critics' views that function is more of a result than a motivation for form and style (interview in Heyer 1966:294–307). Meier too has underplayed function, as was most evident in the court's closing of the Bronx Developmental Center. Complicity in illusion, slippage, and ambiguity of metaphor is what Hubbard (1981) means by "scrim." Richard Meier's works are an apotheoses of scrim: "Meier's houses make us feel good about doing architecture" (Hubbard 1980:221). The themes that bring together Meier and Rudolph are texture, style, surface, and scrim, "rules that allow us to enjoy play" (Hubbard 1980:64). These are the defining characteristics of what Sontag (1967) calls camp, "the sensibility of failed seriousness":

Camp refuses both the harmonies of traditional sensuousness, and the risks of fully identifying with extreme states of feeling. . . . It incarnates a victory of "style" over "content," "aesthetics" over "morality," of irony over tragedy. . . . The whole point of Camp is to dethrone the serious. Camp is playful, anti-serious. More precisely, Camp involves a new, more complex relation to "the serious." One can be serious about the frivolous, frivolous about the serious. (Pp. 287–288.)

Camp, scrim, or if you prefer, mannerist (see C. Ray Smith 1977:333), Rudolph and Meier are interested in wit, elegance, and, above all, sensuality.

In sum, then, we have discovered that older traditions represented by Le Corbusier, Kahn, Wright, and Saarinen are revered, yet they are not directly distinctive in the thinking of working architects. There is a different framework that helps us to understand their convictions. This framework can be described as a set of four independent dimensions: subjectivism versus formalistic, purist, meta-art, and camp. This frame simultaneously reveals both the noetic—the ideas and knowledge that architects have concerning buildings—and the normative—their moral beliefs about buildings as expressions of meanings and functions. By asking about their heroes and rascals, we discover not only their convictions but also what can potentially influence their own work, which is to say influence it in the absence of constraints of the market and of practice.

Astonishing are the implications of the opposition of the subjective, as revealed in the works of Stirling and, particularly, those of Aalto—hermeneutic, vernacularity, and ambiguity—with the formalistic—as evident in the monumental, impersonal, and standardized abstraction of the international style. While critics puzzled over the problem in the mid-1970s of whether the functional movement "had played itself out" (Goldberger 1976b; also see Sobel 1978), rank-and-file architects express here their convictions that it ought to, and they offer an alternative. Yet there is still the possibility that this epistemological analysis yields a better understanding of architects' abstract convictions rather than the more prosaic ones that suffuse their daily work. To explore this possibility, I turn to the analysis of aphoristic quotations.

Aphorisms Expressing Convictions

In order to elicit personal convictions that relate more to architects' own work, thirty-six aphorisms—quotations by architects, planners, and critics—were selected that represent the spectrum of ideas, opinions, and controversies in contemporary architecture. Some of these quotations relate to ideals for design and form (for example, "Texture is extremely important") and others to the process of design (for example, "Buildings should be designed from the inside out, rather than from the outside in"). This difference can lead to some confusion in the initial comparisons of positions that architects tend to support and to reject. In the long run, though, there are certain advantages in combining both types of quotations. The analysis that isolates underlying dimensions demonstrates how certain ideals for design tend to accompany particular positions concerning the process of design. Such connections between what architects think buildings should look like and their ideas about the process of design are otherwise difficult to establish.

For each aphoristic quotation, respondents were asked to indicate whether they strongly agreed, mostly agreed, had no opinion, mostly disagreed, or strongly disagreed. The quotations are ordered in table 4.2 by the combined percentage of strongly agree and agree.

With the exception of item 5, "Texture is extremely important," formal or aesthetic criteria are ranked less highly than social or functional criteria. Generally positions representing the pop school associated with Venturi, such as, "It's good because it's awful" and "Main Street is almost all right," are not, at least among Manhattan architects in 1974, very attractive. Many critics (that is, social science architectural critics) will be surprised to learn how sensitive these architects are to the environment and social functions, as indicated by the positive support given such statements as "Good buildings must relate to their environment" (item 1) and "The aim of architecture should be to restore the 'human scale'—to our buildings, to our cities" (item 7). Each of these positions was endorsed by more than three-quarters of the architects. The aesthetic of contextualism was still a few years off, and it was not until the end of the decade that such statements as "There is a new interest in the context of a building," began to appear in professional journals.[7]

Somewhat inconsistent with the overall pattern is the widely shared conviction, "Spatial relationships can influence, and even determine social relationships" (item 2). Lipman (1969: 190–204) also finds that the belief in architectural determinism is widely shared among British architects. Such strong endorsement of this anachronistic formulation of the relation between environment and behavior indicates architects' general disregard of the large social science literature that demonstrates how complex that relationship is—as people control and restructure their spaces, as cultural definitions and perceptions play a role in the way that individuals behave in environments, as people's social class and other economic, social, and psychological characteristics can override spatial constraints in establishing social relationships (see Zeisel 1975; Gutman 1972; Gans 1968; Lynch 1960; Michelson 1976; Keller 1968; La Gory and Pipkin 1981).

Table 4.2
Amount of agreement with ideas expressed in aphoristic quotations

Quotations	% strongly agree or agree	% no opinion
1. Good buildings must relate to their environment.	95	3
2. Spatial relationships can influence, and even determine, interpersonal social relationships.	86	11
3. Architecture should not be designed for peers or clients but for users.	84	10
4. Much more attention should be given to the users' cultural values, spatial needs, and aesthetic preferences.	84	9
5. Texture is extremely important.	84	10
6. Top priority should be given to the serviceability of buildings: access to transportation, sunlight, public safety, acoustics, and so forth.	81	10
7. The aim of architecture should be to restore the "human scale"—to our buildings, to our cities.	81	12
8. Form follows function.	80	11
9. More than anything, the practitioner requires sound business capability, professional integrity, and the ability to communicate with others.	78	13
10. Every age has its "feelings" and its aspirations. These must be expressed in architecture.	75	16
11. Buildings should be designed from the inside out rather than from the outside in.	68	20
12. Less is more.	60	22
13. Architecture should be the result of a team effort and not the emanation from one isolated ego.	59	15
14. The nature of space reflects what it wants to be.	59	25
15. The really important thing in architecture is proportion.	56	15
16. Buildings should have a sense of humor.	48	31
17. Good design: flair, drama, excitement.	47	20

Table 4.2 (continued)

Quotations	% strongly agree or agree	% no opinion
18. Modern architecture should concern itself with the "recycling" of existing structures, avoiding new structures whenever possible.	46	15
19. We are not interested in architecture as a cultural object or as a status symbol. Anathema to us is the monument in architecture and "prima donna" architect.	44	24
20. A good design must be dynamic.	42	16
21. The best architecture gives one the feeling that it grows out of the soil.	42	23
22. Good design most often is a technical solution.	40	11
23. Honesty is expressed in exposed services—pipes, ducts—and materials.	40	17
24. Good architecture should be a means of advertising.	38	21
25. Monumentality is still a virtue.	38	24
26. We need machines for living instead of cathedrals.	37	21
27. Everyone should be able to build.	29	24
28. Architecture is an affair of the elite.	26	12
29. Less is a bore.	23	31
30. An architect should refuse a commission from the Rhodesian government.	23	28
31. The international style is just too flat-chested.	23	33
32. Main Street is almost all right.	23	34
33. Sociologists don't know anything about how to build. It's only artists who know how.	23	18
34. Who wants to know what the inside looks like from the outside?	16	25
35. What we build will find its usefulness. Form does not follow function.	15	13
36. It's good because it's awful.	5	15

Although a summary of what statements architects tend to endorse provides a worthwhile description of prevailing currents of thinking, it fails to furnish a frame or structure that underlies cognitive and normative orientations. The results of another factor analysis supply the dimensions of that frame (table 4.3).[8] The names I give to these dimensions are *humanist, liberal professional, technical, social responsibility, antiminimalism, antifunctionalism, pragmatic,* and *expressionism.* The first factor is much more important than the others; it accounts for nearly twice the statistical variation than each of the other factors.[9]

The first factor taps humanist concerns and unmistakably indicates the great importance architects attach to what users of buildings want and to the social relevance of design and architectural practice. If architects still are not giving priority to users' needs—and most critics feel they are not—the architects in this study indicate that architects feel this ought to be the case. Whereas the percentage distribution in table 4.2 shows simply

Table 4.3
Dimensions of aphoristic quotations

Factor I: Humanist	
4. Much more attention should be given to the users' cultural values, spatial needs, and aesthetic preferences.	0.57
7. The aim of architecture should be to restore the "human scale"—to our buildings, to our cities.	.55
2. Spatial relationships can influence, and even determine, interpersonal social relationships.	.50
3. Architecture should not be designed for peers or clients but for users.	.50
10. Every age has its "feelings" and its aspirations. These must be expressed in architecture.	.48
14. The nature of space reflects what it wants to be.	.44
1. Good buildings must relate to their environment.	.43
Factor II: Liberal professional	
19. We are not interested in architecture as a cultural object or as a status symbol. Anathema to us is the monument in architecture and the "prima donna" architect.	.54
13. Architecture should be the result of a team effort and not the emanation from one isolated ego.	.46
Factor III: Technical	
22. Good design most often is a technical solution.	.49
23. Honesty is expressed in exposed services—pipes, ducts—and materials.	.47

that many tend to agree, for example, that much more attention should be given to the users' values and preferences and that architecture should not be designed for peers or clients but for users, the greater importance of this first factor reveals that large numbers of architects have the same attitudes about this interrelated set of social issues and that these issues are the most potent and significant.

Prior to the analysis I had expected that the quotations indicating a concern with users would be part of a larger pattern and include the items that deal with the progressive practice of architecture, specifically an interest in team practice (item 13) and the anti-elitism expressed in item 19, which includes the statement, "Anathema to us is the monument in architecture and the 'prima donna' architect." This is not the case. The progressive orientation to architectural practice that underlies these items is important, but it is quite distinct (statistically independent) from the humanistic perspective. Both items (13 and 19) load high on the second factor, liberal professional.

Table 4.3 (continued)

Factor IV: Social responsibility	
30. An architect should refuse a commission from the Rhodesian government.	.49
16. Buildings should have a sense of humor.	.44
18. Modern architecture should concern itself with the "recycling" of existing structures, avoiding new structures whenever possible.	.41
Factor V: Antiminimalism	
29. Less is a bore.	.88
12. Less is more.	−.55
Factor VI: Antifunctionalism	
35. What we build will find its usefulness. Form does not follow function.	.70
8. Form follows function.	−.58
Factor VII: Pragmatic	
6. Top priority should be given to the serviceability of buildings: access to transportation, sunlight, public safety, acoustics, and so forth.	.64
9. More than anything, the practitioner requires sound business capability, professional integrity, and the ability to communicate with others.	.60
Factor VIII: Expressionism	
17. Good design: flair, drama, excitement.	.61
20. A good design must be dynamic.	.54

The technical dimension (factor III) brings together two related concerns: the view that design and technical problems are one and the same and an emphasis on exposed services (pipes, stairs, and so forth) as stressed by brutalism, for example. Generally this factor reflects a straightforward approach to materials and technology.

The fourth factor is especially interesting for it is comprised of items whose similarity is not obvious. What they appear to have in common is the principle that architecture must serve ends that are not merely architectural but are politically relevant as well. The ethical responsibility of the architect is the underlying theme; ethics here encompasses social commentary, as well as the architectural joke.

The negative pole of the first dimension of the factor analysis of architectural heroes (formalism) is similar to the negative factor loadings on the fifth and sixth factors of the analysis of quotations, antiminimalism and antifunctionalism. The style that dominated design practice—what I have termed formalism—faces large opposition within the architectural community. It is possible, however, that eminent individuals are more likely to engender schools of opposition than are the ideas they represent. This is argued on the grounds that opposition to the works of Yamasaki, Stone, and Harrison seems to be better organized, for the negative factor loadings of formalism are represented by a more important factor (it accounts for more of the variance) than opposition to the ideal with which they are associated. It may be generally true that in a period of intellectual ferment—in science, academia, or art—opinions become mobilized against individuals who stand for the older tradition but not so much against the old as for a new set of ideals.

The pragmatic orientation (factor VII) includes both the idea that buildings should be practical to live in and the idea that the architect must possess the sensible virtues of a successful but enlightened entrepreneur. The more romantic image of the architect—neurotic, egoistic, creative—is denied by this definition.

There is only one factor revealing advocacy for a particular design aesthetic that accounts for any significant proportion of the variation in the responses: expressionism, factor VIII. Since other design-related statements (for example, "Texture is extremely important" and "The really important thing in architecture is proportion") were not sufficiently salient to be included in the factor solution, this indicates that the formal attributes revealed by factor VIII—"flair, drama, excitement" and "dynamic" qualities—represent the only design aesthetic that has a clear integrity or viability. This may be an indication of future developments in architecture, particularly since this factor is somewhat parallel to the subjectivism pole of the first factor in the analysis of heroes and rascals.

In conclusion, this further exploration of architects' working convictions strongly indicates that some of the most important issues in architecture do not pertain to questions of design and form but rather to those of the human use of buildings and the social qualities of architecture. Yet the high regard in which the concept of architectural determinism is held raises some question about the logic that motivates architects' expressed convictions concerning humane architecture. There is a lack of logic when architects believe that users' values, needs, and preferences ought to be taken into account in an architecture that determines those values, needs, and preferences. There may be a hint of imperialism and professional protectionism lurking here. The results suggest that architects, despite their social awareness, are not very receptive to the findings of social research. Indeed Kevin Roche, an architect of very many humane buildings, says, "Sociology would be a good idea, but it is not very useful" (quoted in Cook and Klotz 1973:55).

Agendas of Firm Heads

Because of the multiple character of professional firms— obligations to the client and the public, market context, legal restrictions, organizational relationships, internal organization, and standards for project design—the agendas for the firm, as established by its principal, rest on many considerations. Meadows (1983:41), in describing agendas for such offices, writes, "Some of them are official, overt, precise, clear; others often remain murkily ambiguous, even unstated." Agendas serve to justify and to legitimize firm activities, and they provide a link between values and the decision-making process (Beyer 1982).

To provide a context for the study of architects' convictions about built architecture, I asked the principals of firms who were personally interviewed in 1974 about their agendas for their office's projects. Specifically they were asked, "How do you define a successful project that is done in your office? What, in other words, do you aim for in your work?" This question was asked again in 1979 in the telephone interview.[10] At both times most principals discussed their agendas for their work in terms of multiple criteria, although the telephone interviews elicited less detailed responses; the 1979 interviews obtained information on the single criterion that principals emphasized as most important. Answers were coded in terms of the categories reported in table 4.4.

It is clear that economic criteria (item 1) and the satisfaction of clients (item 2) dominate these principals' concerns in both the mid- and late 1970s. Substantial numbers at both times men-

Table 4.4
Principal's firm agendas

Category	1974		1979
	% mentioned	% emphasized	% mentioned
1. Financially successful	69	19	70
2. Client satisfaction	65	25	52
3. Aesthetically or architecturally exciting	49	16	20
4. Design adheres to aesthetic objective	37	11	30
5. Personally satisfied	32	7	18
6. Logical and functional	29	3	17
7. Serves people's needs	25	8	16
8. Have no major problem with client, owner, or contractors	21	1	12
9. Project contributes to architectural thinking; brings professional recognition	13	0	10
10. Project improves with use	7	0	0
11. Project continues to give pleasure	5	0	2
12. No compromises from the firm's point of view	4	0	1
13. Project demonstrates how architecture can improve life; project educates client or the public	4	0	0

tioned aesthetic criteria (items 3, 4, 6), although 30 percent emphasized them. About 40 percent of the principals mentioned the social functions or the socially enduring qualities of projects in 1974 (items 7, 10, and 11 combined), but fewer did in 1979—only about 20 percent. Professional reputation and personal gratification (items 5, 9) are mentioned by 45 percent of the firm heads in the initial interview and by 28 percent of them in the later survey.

Although priorities among the agendas of the heads of offices are relatively stable over the five-year period, some substantial shifts are evident between 1974 and 1979. To be sure, four items—"financially successful" and "client satisfaction" and the two major office agendas, architectural expressionism (implied by category 3) and functionalism (implied by category 4)—are the ones most stressed in both years. The emphases on the criteria are different, however. For example, although about the same percentage of firm heads mention financial success in both years, there is a much greater stress on this in 1979 compared with the second most frequently mentioned criterion, client satisfaction. That is, although financial success and client satisfaction are mentioned in 1974 by 69 percent and 65 percent, respectively, in 1979, 70 percent mention financial success and 52 percent mention client satisfaction. Aside from this shift in priorities, considerably fewer in 1979, compared with 1974, mention design criteria. In 1974 categories 3 and 4 combined are mentioned by 85 percent of all firm heads, which is considerably more than the 50 percent in 1979.

Thus the agendas of firm heads reveal, understandably enough, highly pragmatic attitudes concerning projects. They become increasingly so as the straits of firms generally worsened over these five years. Much further removed from the agendas of firm heads than from the convictions of rank-and-file architects is a concern with users, the environmental context of buildings, and the social functions of architecture. Yet the general lack of arrogance among both employees and managers is of interest. For example, few principals conceived their mission to be one with "no compromises" or to be one of "educating the client or the public," and practically none conceived it in these terms at the end of the decade. This is hardly proof, but nevertheless indicative, that the Howard Roark image (architect as arrogant individualist) is not a particularly apt reference for architects now (for a different interpretation, see Saint 1983).

Conclusions

The ideas of working architects are precociously ahead of their buildings and are barely in accordance with firm agendas, which are attuned to the practicality of architecture. In this sense architects are slow radicals. We have examined too the premise of specificity, which in its most general formulation states that art is isolated and independent of the sociohistorical context. But quite the contrary, built architecture appears to accommodate rather well to its context. Contemporary urban towers continue to symbolize the power of corporate and state elites; flats built in slums label the poor impoverished; plazas mandated by urban governments most often end up as providing more pizzazz than genuine amenities; and although developers are responsible for most suburbs, the most pretentious and segregated often come from some architect's drafting table. None of this is new. What is new is to discover that the working architect holds convictions quite different from the premises behind such a built environment. Relative to praxis, architects' convictions exhibit features of specificity. This itself puts the profession under conditions of risk because of the contradictions between praxis and ideas.

I have hinted that firms' agendas, which mediate between architecture as commerce and architecture as building, mute the convictions of rank-and-file architects. This is not quite correct, for there is some degree of correspondence between agendas of the firm head and convictions of architects who work in that office. For example, when financial criteria are emphasized, the dominant heroes in the firm are Neutra, Niemeyer, and Nervi (technical purity leads to some quite costly buildings); an agenda of client satisfaction accompanies antiminimalism (for example, as indicated by the statement, "Less is a bore"); and, the third and fourth dimensions of agenda that pertain to aesthetics are found in firms whose architects admire Stirling and Aalto and endorse the liberal professional ideology that emphasizes team design. [11] Therefore convictions of architects are not inconsistent with agendas of their immediate work context, although the way that architects prioritize design criteria is very different from the way that the heads of firms prioritize what is important for a project as it relates to the organization. Convictions are idealistic, whereas agendas are eminently practical and pragmatic.

These considerations bring us to the next problem, an examination of the links joining convictions and agendas, the material base and organization of practice, and design quality.

5

The Eccentricity of Merit

The explication of genius and creativity is traditionally, and still predominantly, sought in the special nature of the individual. This is true of scholarly accounts of scientific enterprise (Zuckerman 1975; Sarton 1957) and certainly so for the arts (Santayana 1955; Wind 1969; Cary 1958; Deinhard 1970), the two principal fields for which creativity is of central importance. The chronicles of architecture deal nearly exclusively with the character of the individual genius: their minds (Summerson 1963), intensity (Schuyler 1964), passions (Pevsner 1960), competitiveness (Huizinga 1955), and biographies (Hitchcock 1968). Architectural history, according to Watkin (1977:113), is built on genius, "the creative, mysterious, and unpredictable"; he rejects both the sociological explanation that rests on the analyses of influences of social conditions and the cultural explanation that emphasizes societal values.

There are two points to be made here. The first is quite simple, the second more complicated, requiring a comparison of the approach used in architectural history and criticism with that used in social science. First, I contend that the notion of individual genius is something of a romantic anachronism, a view shared by Boyle (1977), Saint (1983), and Muschamp (1974). My interviews with architects made it clear that design responsibilities are often shared, and for a complex project many specialists collaborate, as was noted more than twenty years ago by Norberg-Schulz (1963). I therefore consider creative products, not creative individuals, and examine the conditions in the firm, not the characteristics of designers, in this analysis of merit.

The second point involves the great differences between the approach employed by social scientists and that by students of art or architecture, and it has direct bearing on why I measure quality the way I do and why I proceed with an explanation of it. Watkin (1977:62), who considers sociologists' approach "vulgar," shares with some others in the humanities the false impression that the aim of social science explanation is to reduce something of intrinsic interest—say, architectural style—to other factors—social class, cultural values, architects' training. On the contrary, the aim is to show that the social conditions in which architectural styles (for example) develop influence the nature of these developments. Further, it is assumed that creativity is necessary but not sufficient for merit because other factors play a role. In contrast the dominant mode of analysis in architectural history and criticism is interpretation, which reveals the essence or inherent qualities of the phenomena (Whitehead 1925). To be sure there is some overlap since interpretation, the prototype of humanistic analysis, has played an important role in social philosophy, as illustrated by Weber's (1946) concept of *verstehen,* which is usually translated as interpretive or empathetic understanding. An explanatory or propositional social science has influenced recent developments in history, as have empirical techniques been used in the study of aesthetic perceptions. Nevertheless there is a traditional difference between the way that humanist scholars approach problems and the way that social scientists do, which deserves some elaboration.

To take a current and concrete example, semiotic analysis, which is not of major concern for most social scientists, has had an electrifying effect in humanistic disciplines. Although more specific (as a theory) than interpretation (a general mode of understanding), it rests on the same assumption: that there is an ongoing, uninterrupted process and synthetic whole. This is very different from the assumption behind explanation or propositional knowledge, for which sets of phenomena are independently defined and the relations among them are explained by theoretical propositions.

In semiotics the signifier (the building) and the signified (the concept expressed by the signifier) together have the same identity, as sign. The signified is the meaning, conception, code, or image conveyed by the signifier, and it carries a variety of connotations—cognitive and expressive, normative and symbolic. Yet neither signifier nor signified has an independent existence; the two are inseparable as the holistic experience of architectural sign; signified and signifier can be defined or analyzed only in relation to each other. Whereas explanational knowledge is valued when it is parsimonious and focused, interpretative knowledge, semiotics providing the example, is avaricious in its range of concerns and synthetic in its logic. For example, Winner (1978:335) maintains, "Meaning and change [are] inseparable from cultural structure or systems. . . . [The aim] is to search for a common perspective that will unite all human behavior within a general framework." In short everything is relevant at once, which is why interpretation has such appeal for the historian or critic, whose aim is to communicate the true measure and significance of feeling and ideas.

Interestingly the process of creation follows the same path. The transformational synthesis involved in creativity has been described by many artists and scientists. P. F. Smith (1974:238), an English architect, puts it particularly well: "Architects use forms and materials as symbols: the interaction between context [style and emotion] and symbol is a circular process. . . . to anyone engaged in any form or creativity, nothing is irrelevant. . . . a highly rational, deductive, unyielding mind does not offer sufficient fissures in its hard crust for the fruits of bisociation to break through. It cannot possess the 'eureka' act."

This connection between the paradigm of interpretation and the eureka act of creativity is important for several reasons. First, it indicates the integrity of architectural products—that they somehow begin as synthetic wholes and are evaluated in the same way. Sociologists who study art tend to see it in this way too. Art, sociologist Manfredi (1982:4) writes, "does not fall apart as a separate universe of discourse or analysis (as does, for instance, juvenile delinquency)." This is not trivial, for I am suggesting here, in agreement with both Watkin and Manfredi, that the merit of buildings cannot be explained, only evaluated within a framework of interpretation based on judgments that come from insiders' intuitions (Seitz 1969). Thus professionals must be relied on for assessments of quality. Second, this connection between interpretation and creativity suggests how the problem of merit will be approached here. My purpose is to examine how conditions in the firm and how ideas of architects (convictions and agendas) together help to account for why some firms produce more innovative design than others. To explain creative work is not to explain it away but rather to provide an understanding of its context.

Measuring Merit

Doctrinal differences that emerged within the architectural community in the mid-1970s, as revealed most clearly by the polarity of convictions and also by the waffling of critics as to the directions in which architecture was headed, might indicate that the criteria for evaluation were in disarray too. Paradoxically this is not—and cannot be—the case. Even in the absence of orthodoxy in any profession, members of the professional community tend to agree about quality. Although they may argue about style, technique, and approach, they nevertheless produce reliable judgments about what is good and therefore worthy of attention (Becker 1982; see also Hershberger 1969; Etzkorn 1973; Virgil Thomson 1969).

If professional colleagues could not agree on standards, there would be no professional community; it would succumb to doctrinal differences that often exist with respect to style, approach, and technique or, perhaps more serious, would yield under the superimposition of standards of outsiders (engineers, sociologists, planners). What is said in derision—"architects work for other architects"—is exactly the point. Only within the profession are the same canonical standards about excellence shared.

To be sure, the possibility exists that the premature discoverer may not be recognized by colleagues at the time (for example, Adolph Loos, Charles Ives, Samuel Beckett, Gregor Mendel) and so does the possibility that the reputations of the once eminent are later reassessed (Herbert Spencer, Adolphe Bouguereau, and Daniel Burnham are cases in point). Although history may not support the judgments that are made, the prevailing standards of merit are canonical in the sense that there are strong structures that link the convictions of what is worthwhile (creative, novel, innovative) with empirical instances of it (see Stent 1972). This view of quality draws attention to the fact that professional standards are based on insiders' judgments that are consensual but also recognizes that they may not be consistent with the judgments of their successors or with those of the public.

To measure quality, I turn therefore to various sources of collegial evaluations. First, all of the faculty members teaching in each of the five New York City schools of architecture were mailed a questionnaire asking them to evaluate the products of

the various firms. A second measure is the number of times the
work of a firm had been reviewed in professional journals during the preceding five-year period.[1] The third is the combined
number of awards received and competitions won during the
preceding five-year period.[2] (Because entering and winning
competitions is not as frequent as award winning, this measure is
simply referred to as awards.)

The three measures are highly related, which supports the
assumption that standards are largely shared and that the different sources of collegial evaluation yield the same results.[3] It
also indicates that no measure is inherently better than the
others. The choice could be made on methodological grounds.
The awards measure was selected over the other two for the
following reasons. The response rate of the faculty was only
about 50 percent, which makes this a less reliable measure than
the other two. One problem with journal articles is they sometimes cite an architect without indicating whether the architect is
attached to a firm; further the conferral of credit in journals is
delayed by lead time and printing. The awards measure is superior to either faculty evaluations or journals for these reasons.
Another advantage it offers is that the jury selection for awards
was fairly diffuse by the mid-1970s and often included nonelite
architects.[4] The indication of outstanding merit, then, is the
number of awards the firm had received over a five-year period,
1969 through 1973.

Architects may still raise objections about the way I measure
reputed merit. Politics, a tendency of juries to choose the conventional over the daring, and the notorious role of old-boy
networks in the selection process contribute to some wariness
in the architectural community about the meaningfulness of
awards and competitions. The same unease is expressed within
the community of performers about the reliability of the Tony
and Obie awards. Yet juried awards provide the best measuring
stick available for the purpose of comparing many firms, just as
theatrical awards would be a fairly good indicator of relative
differences in the reputation or achieved merit of performers.
There is also the advantage in the award measure in that it is not
heavily biased by one or several juries since many awards and
competitions are included, and it is not a reflection of very
short-lived reputations since the information spans five years.
Just as academicians have learned to live with citation counts as

the indicator of the relative worth of achievements because they can find no better, I employ the number of awards with the same motivation: there is none that is demonstrably superior to it.

Agendas, Convictions, and Merit

It seems plausible to assume that agendas and convictions would have manifest compatibility and logical outcomes. Indeed agendas of firm heads and the convictions of architects do exhibit some correspondence so that when, for example, the head of a firm emphasizes design merit over efficiency, staff architects tend to espouse a subjectivist approach rather than one of formalism associated with the international style.

Yet there are no apparent connections between either agendas or convictions, on the one hand, and quality, on the other. The correlation between an agenda of aesthetics and winning awards is negligible ($r = 0.03$), and so is the one between subjectivism and awards ($r = 0.03$). Neither is it the case that an emphasis on profits is negatively related to awards ($r = 0.09$), and although client satisfaction is negatively related to quality ($r = -0.17$), the relationship is small and not significant.

This might suggest that ideas are inconsequential. Alternatively it is possible that the effects of ideas are concealed by other factors and conditions.[5] For this analysis I identify main parameters of firm organization and employ them to test whether they disclose the significance of ideas for merit. The analysis of agendas is limited to the seventy-seven firms in which I asked the question about what principals consider a successful project. The analysis of convictions is based on 310 individuals, with each being characterized both by his or her convictions and by the characteristics of the firm in which the person works.[6]

Client Satisfaction
In those firms for which there is an emphasis on client satisfaction, there is no greater or lesser likelihood of award winning. Only when this orientation to clients is embedded in a particular organizational form does it become significantly antithetical to merited work. In the most general terms the negative influence of a client orientation is contingent on a set of rationalized and bureaucratic features:[7]

Agenda of client satisfaction ——————→ *Awards*
Under the conditions of:
Incorporated
Many joint ventures
Large size
Many local projects

Such firms are also likely to have many local commissions, which is consistent with an emphasis on clients since proximity fosters closer client ties (just as an emphasis on close client ties also fosters a preference for local projects). Thus a preoccupation with client satisfaction in itself is not deleterious to award winning, but it is so under particular conditions: those of marked bureaucratic rationality. Under these conditions, such a preoccupation detracts attention from award-winning design work.

Mitchell (1974) cited James Ackerman as saying there are two schools of thought among architects: "Give um what they want" and "give them what I want." When the former school of thought dominates in the context of a bureaucratic—large, corporate—firm, the products of the firm take on a pedestrian quality (though, of course, they may very well be appreciated by the client).

Profits
A main interest in financial success is surprisingly unrelated to merit, although when this interest is accompanied by certain structural features of the firm, it becomes detrimental for award winning. When an orientation to profit-making is inset in a firm with a disproportionate number of corporate clients, and mostly local commissions, the firm is unlikely to produce high-quality work:[8]

Agenda of profit-making ——————→ *Awards*
Under the conditions of:
Corporate clients
Many local projects
Staff decline in 1973
Survival

The possibility exists that an emphasis on making profits develops out of economic hardship, which is indicated here by staff reductions in 1973. Such reductions are in fact consistent with a profit orientation and not winning awards, which suggests that financial difficulties increase concern with economic efficiency and endanger the quality of architectural work as the attempt is made to cut corners. Yet the other possibility is that firms in which financial criteria are very important are most likely to take swift action and to fire staff during periods of economic difficulties. In the long run these firms did well; they were more likely to survive over the next five years. Thus economic rationality appears to hinder high quality primarily among firms that have a corporate clientele and whose mode of operation, being consistent with theirs, emphasizes careful cost accounting in employment policies. Such a combination results in considerable tenacity in periods of recession.

Aesthetics
The particular orientation regarding aesthetics has no consequence for quality design without taking into account other factors. When it is combined with certain firm characteristics, it becomes positively linked with merit:[9]

Agenda of aesthetics $\xrightarrow{\quad + \quad}$ *Awards*
Under the conditions of:
Unaffiliated
Few engineers
Diverse services

   The firm characteristics that enable such an orientation to become instrumental for winning design awards are the following: the office's autonomy from other firms (that is, its not being a subsidiary, a branch, or an affiliate), a high percentage of architects (with a correspondingly low percentage of engineers and technicians), and diverse client services. This set of conditions, which provides an affinity between a strong design orientation and awards, is different in character from those that provide disaffinities in the case of either a profit or a client orientation. They are different in that they do not deal with economic rationality or organizational rationality; rather they pertain to the professional nature of the firm. Each of these factors taps particular aspects of the autonomous professional firm, not the corporate or the business firm.

Convictions

The main dimension that summarizes architects' convictions is bipolar—subjectivism versus formalism—rather than a set of independent dimensions, as is the case for the agendas of firm heads. Architects who espouse subjectivism (whose heroes are Stirling and Aalto) actively reject formalism (and their rascals are Yamasaki, Stone, Harrison, Speer, and Lapidus); the reverse is also true. To simplify this analysis, I classified all individuals into subjectivists and formalists using their scores on this first factor. The number classified as subjectivists is 150 and the number who are formalists is 160. Although there is every reason to suppose that subjectivists—the aesthetic progressives— are more likely to work in firms that produce award-winning projects, this is not so simply the case. The simple correlation between subjectivism (which describes the orientations of the individual architect) and her or his firm's winning awards is −.06. Yet further analyses indicate that there also exists a set of structural conditions that mediate between architects' convictions and quality to reveal a logical connection between ideas and outcomes:

$$\textit{Convictional subjectivism} \xrightarrow{\ +\ } \textit{Awards}$$

Under the conditions of:
Young firm
Few corporate clients
Unbureaucratic

$$\textit{Convictional formalism} \xrightarrow{\ -\ } \textit{Awards}$$

Under the conditions of:
Older firm
Many corporate clients
Bureaucratic

Individual architects who are strongly identified with subjectivism are far more likely to work in award-winning firms but only when those firms have certain characteristics. These firms are relatively young, have few corporate clients, and are little bureaucratized, that is, have few written rules.[10] Architects who espouse formalist principles in design are less likely to work in award-winning firms but this is only because their firms tend to be long established, have many corporate clients, and are highly bureaucratized.

Thus a connection between architects' convictions and merit exists but only when appropriate conditions prevail in the firm; without those conditions what architects believe to be important for design make no difference for whether the firm excels in terms of prevailing standards of merit. The office in which rank-and-file architects are oriented to progressive design schools that I have termed subjectivism is likely to win awards but only if the firm is relatively young, has few corporate clients, and is notably unbureaucratic. These firm characteristics are similar, though not identical, to those revealed in the analysis of an agenda of aesthetics; they signify main features of the professional, entrepreneurial office, as distinct from the large streamlined and rationalized corporation. The office in which rank-and-file architects are bound to convictions that emphasize impersonal and formalistic design standards are less likely to win awards when that office has particular characteristics. When what I have called formalism prevails in a firm that is relatively old, depends on corporate clients for most of their commissions, and is bureaucratic, the firm is unlikely to win awards. In this way ideas are consequential for winning awards but only when they are wedded to certain structural conditions. There are, then, logical connections between ideas and outcomes, but these connections are disclosed only when features of social context facilitate and mediate the linkages.

Recapitulation: Ideas and Material Conditions

It is a set of characteristics that betoken the traditional entrepreneurial firm—autonomy, an emphasis on architecture rather than engineering, and diverse professional services—that provides the connection linking a core professional value, an agenda of aesthetics, and merit. In contrast what impairs the ability of offices to win awards when either clients or profits are emphasized by the head of the firm is a narrowly rational business structure. The distinctive feature that is responsible for the negative effect of an agenda of profitability on merit is preoccupation with economic rationality; the one that establishes the negative effect of an agenda of client satisfaction is preoccupation with organizational rationality. Thus offices that have as their main goals agendas geared to market principles will fail to live up to professional standards of quality when their structures are consistent with those goals.

When architects endorse subjectivism—which was the paradigm of progressivism and experimentation in the mid-1970s—the firm is more likely to win awards as long as the firm is neither organized along strictly rational lines nor dependent on major capitalistic markets. Thus only when there is a logical connection between agenda or convictions and work environments are professional objectives likely to be realized.

One must be wary of the implications of these results. Due to the wide variation in characteristics within firms, there is not a great chance of simultaneous compatible interlock between both agenda and convictions, on the one hand, and firm conditions on the other. The characteristics of firms on which the linkage between subjectivism and winning awards depends are not the only characteristics of firms that are likely to win awards.

A conclusion that is problematic for the profession relates to the finding that the only patterned set of firm characteristics that includes survival is found in firms in which profits are emphasized and that have inferior reputations. The political economy model of organizations is clearly relevant here: firms with a calculative approach to professional staffing and a dependence on corporate clients have a competitive edge in the marketplace but may do poorly in producing high-quality products. These are not encouraging results. Of course, it is possible that there is a steady replacement of high-quality firms that fail to survive in the oligopolistic market by new firms, which may be similarly ill equipped in the market yet have fresh design approaches. Such a replacement would maintain a balance between the core and the periphery, between profit-seeking firms and those with a lively interest in quality design.

Firm Structure and Awards

Only when linked with particular structural features do firm agendas and architects' convictions become consequential for award winning. But this analysis fails to put into proper perspective the significance of firm structure for the central and most critical point is that large firms tend to win many awards and small ones tend to win few. This relationship is so pronounced that it initially appears that hardly anything else could matter. This discussion, though, will show that although large scale counts for a great deal, so do the peculiar features evident only in small offices.

The most consistent idea I encountered on the topic of organizational characteristics and high-quality work in the interviews is that the small or medium-sized office does the best work. Even when, in architects' views, large size is advantageous, say, for recruitment of talented architects and for securing big commissions, much that accompanies large size is, as they perceive it, disadvantageous for quality. These adjunct features of large scale, they believe, include too much specialization, a reduced ability to keep track of the project, and the likelihood of communication breakdowns. The comparison architects make between the production firm and the design firm is nearly always related to difference in size. After pointing out that large firms are more interested in production that in design, one respondent added, "When I think of the architects around the world who are well known, for one reason or another, almost without exception all of them have medium-sized offices. Corbu's was, and so is Tange's." Another architect emphasized the flexibility of the smaller office as an advantage. In general, although architects accept modern accounting procedures, the use of specialists, such as engineers, and the complex relations with outsiders entailed in consulting and joint ventures, there is a general suspicion of a congeries of office characteristics that I have described as the ones underlying the rationalization and routinization of practice, notably much subdivision, specialization, and formalization of rules.

Although critics tend to deplore the effects of corporate clients on the integrity of office practice (see Mumford 1947, 1959; Andrews 1964; Colbert 1966; Fitch 1966), architects I interviewed are more equivocal about whether powerful corporate clients corrupt the creative component of architecture. One architect suggests that they must be handled differently from other clients: "You can be disadvantaged dealing with the corporate client, particularly if you have to deal with several people or a committee. That reduces your autonomy. But if you set up the guidelines at the beginning . . . if you let that be your working principle . . . you have a lot of autonomy, about design, I mean." An architect who steers clear of corporate commissions said, "You can do the most exciting work with the private individual or business client, because there is continuous interaction." Some complained most about government commissions because of red tape, although I also heard the opposite view: "More often than not, the government would prefer to have something good rather than not good." And there were many comments to the effect that if the firm specializes in a particular type of client for a long period of time, the firm can turn stale.

Partnerships, too, for a variety of reasons, including their superior flexibility and methods for maintaining accountability, were considered by many of the architects I interviewed as being most capable of doing high-quality work.

Correlates of Quality
These views about what makes a firm likely to do superior projects are hypotheses about the relationships between organizational characteristics and quality. Many of them, however, are counter to theory and research an organizational innovation. There is, for example, strong evidence that the more complex an organization is, all other things being equal, the more likely it is to develop innovative products or novel solutions to problems because of the lively exchange of ideas among different specialists (J. Q. Wilson 1966; Aiken and Hage 1968; Moch and Morse 1977; Hage 1980). In general large organizations are found to do higher-quality work than small ones, partly because of their greater complexity (P. M. Blau 1973) and partly because some types of innovation require vast and expensive resources, which is the case in science, for example (J. Blau 1976a).

The simple correlations between awards and firm characteristics are reported in table 5.1. At first it appears that neither the professional lore has much truth to it, nor is the specific sociological hypothesis—that much complexity fosters quality or innovation—supported. Size is highly related to winning awards, and although complexity is positively related to awards, it is not statistically significant. The results indicate that partnerships are slightly advantaged, as many architects mentioned, but so are affiliated firms, offices that are part of a corporation or a subsidiary of one. Every indicator of formalization (operating rules, personnel regulation, and a computer technology) is substantially and positively related to awards, and so is office age, contrary to architects' expectation that new design ideas originate in young offices and also contrary to the thinking of sociologists on the question of organizational age and innovation (Steiner 1965). Counter to the implications of the contrast between design and production firms, with the former's presumed dependence on a highly qualified professional staff being responsible for its superior work, it seems to be those firms with a low proportion of architects and a correspondingly high proportion of technicians that tend to win awards.

The frequent use of other professional firms, either as consultants on projects or in joint ventures with them, also is related to the chances that a firm will win awards. Again, in contrast to what architects expect, neither the type of predominant client nor whether clients are of few or of many types makes much of a difference for awards, with the exception that having many private clients slightly reduces it. High productivity, in contrast, is quite highly correlated with quality.

Theoretically size is antecedent to other organizational characteristics (see P. Blau and Schoenherr 1971), and because of its

Table 5.1
Correlations between firm characteristics and awards, partial correlations controlling for size, and correlations between firm characteristics and size

	Simple correlations with awards	Partial correlations controlling size	Simple correlations with size
Firm type			
Partnership	.16*	.01	.19*
Corporation	.06	−.12	.32**
Affiliate	.27**	.07	.42**
Internal features			
Complexity	.13	−.29**	.40**
Operating rules	.24**	.00	.46**
Personnel regulations	.26**	−.02	.54**
Percentage architects	−.17*	.27**	−.67**
Computer	.40**	−.08	.40**
Age	.25**	−.01	.50**
Relations with other firms and clients			
Has joint ventures	.23**	.06	.35**
Uses consultants	.19**	−.00	.39**
Many comprehensive services	.23*	.04	.51**
Diverse clients	.05	−.11	.28**
Many private clients	−.13*	.05	−.35**
Many corporate clients	.11	.05	.13*
Many government clients	.00	−.10	.04
Productivity	.22**	.06	.33**
Firm size (log)	.51**		

Note: The number of cases is between 145 and 152, except for complexity, which is 95.
*Significant at .05 level.
**Significant at .01 level.

extraordinarily high relationship with quality, it is important to control size statistically to determine whether other characteristics make a marginal difference if all organizations had the same size (which is, in effect, what holding size statistically constant simulates). These results are reported in table 5.1. To help interpret these partial correlations, the simple correlations between firm size and other firm characteristics are also reported.

The results in column 2 indicate that most of the characteristics related to awards are no longer related when size is held constant. These features do accompany quality, but the reason is that they are characteristic of the large office just as is winning awards, and after size is taken into account, they have no causal significance. For example, large offices tend to have more bureaucratic and formalized features, such as rules, personnel regulations, and a computer, as is evident in column 3, and this is the explanation for why they are associated with winning awards. To recall an earlier example, the explanation for why there is a high birthrate in Swedish towns that have large populations of storks is that small towns tend to attract storks and families living in such towns tend to have more children than families in big towns. Similarly firms that are very bureaucratic tend to win many awards, but the explanation is not that bureaucracy promotes meritorious work but rather that big firms are inevitably bureaucratic, and their large size has intrinsic advantages for high-quality project design.

Yet two important characteristics of large firms tend to disadvantage them. First, they are likely to hire disproportionately fewer trained architects and proportionately more technicians and other support staff. While this practice unquestionably achieves savings in salaries and benefits the architectural staff because it relieves them of routine work, it simultaneously handicaps that firm. Independent of size, the higher the proportion of architects on the staff, the higher the quality of the firm's work. Second, firm complexity, indicated by many departments, is also negatively related to winning awards, which is consistent with the opinion of architects that much fragmentation impedes quality but inconsistent with sociological studies of organizational innovation. Many divisions are, in fact, the main trait of the departmentalized office, which is subdivided by tasks rather than by project. This arrangement is the least satisfactory for staff members because it reduces their morale and enthusiasm for work. Here we find that this office form is likely to reduce the overall quality of project design.

Large firms are normally advantaged with the exception of their excessive reliance on technicians and their tendency to departmentalize, both of which somewhat reduce their likelihood of winning awards. We have also seen that when an agenda of client satisfaction becomes prominent in a large office that has other features normally associated with size, specifically incorporation and many joint ventures, its inherent advantages for merit will be lost.

Normally Disadvantaged Firms
Many correlations between awards and other firm characteristics are spurious; when size is taken into account, most firm conditions have no causal influence on awards. In table 5.1 only two factors—complexity and percentage architects—were found to have an influence on awards independent of size, as is evident in that they remain related to awards when size is held constant. Additional tabular analyses reveal, however, that there are important differences between small firms (with fewer than eight full-time staff, the median of raw size) and larger firms.[11] Small firms that are structurally eccentric are much more likely to win awards. Large firms, in contrast, are normally advantaged; when they have characteristics out of keeping with their size, they are rarely hurt or particularly advantaged by them.

The percentage of small firms that win awards is only 33 percent, compared with 71 percent for large firms. All of the characteristics listed in table 5.2 are ones that are typical of large, not small, firms (with the exception of government clients). Each firm attribute is listed along with the percentage of small firms that have it and the percentage having the attribute that wins awards.[12]

Each of these large-firm traits, when acquired —against expected odds—by the small office, improves its chances of winning awards, sometimes dramatically so, as in the case of affiliation, complexity, personnel regulations, consultants, and government clients. Even the small firm that is atypical in being unusually productive is more likely to win awards than the normal small firm, the typical one that is not so productive.

Some of these findings help to explain the origins of professional lore. The small firm that is a partnership rather than the

Table 5.2
Percentage of small firms with given characteristic and percentage of ones with these characteristics that win awards

	Percentage with given characteristic	Percentage winning award
Corporation	8	83
Partnership	24	44
Affiliate	16	53
Complex	22	67
Many operating rules	31	46
Personnel regulations	24	56
Many nonarchitects	17	46
Computer	9	43
Older firm	20	40
Uses consultants	28	48
Many comprehensive services	34	46
Diverse clients	39	44
Many government clients	33	52
Productive	37	46
Percentage of all small firms that win awards		33

Note: Award winning is having won at least one award in the five years preceding this study. All other noncategorical variables are divided at their medians. The smallest N is for complexity (40) because the tiny firms do not have divisions. Ns for the other variables are between 74 and 76.

more typical sole proprietorship tends to excel, and these findings substantiate architects' belief that the office ought to do a great diversity of work rather than specialize in one type of client or project type. Yet in support of sociological research and in opposition to architects' notions about complexity, I find that differentiation is a great advantage for the smaller firms (whereas contrary to sociological research and in support of architects' notions, the more complex the large office, the less noteworthy is its work).

In general, then, excellence in design is not impaired by bureaucratic rationalization. With the exception of complexity, such bureaucratic features as rules do not hurt the work of the large firm, and they improve quality as long as they occur when acquired by offices prematurely, while they are still small. And if bureaucratization does not reduce quality, no single structural variable that signals engulfment by corporate rationality and corporate markets is found to corrupt the work of the small firm.

Question of Stability

More high-quality firms tended to survive the economic recession than low-quality firms. The offices that went bankrupt or left the city averaged about half the number of awards (about one per firm between 1969 and 1974) than those that stayed (about three per firm for the same period). In general the same patterns persist in 1979 that I have described for 1974. Large firms are far more likely than small firms to win awards, but small firms that do exhibit eccentric features are also likely to excel. For example, small firms that employed excessively large numbers of technicians or had many comprehensive services or diverse clients—atypical practices for their size—won far more awards in 1979 than their conventional counterparts. Thus the characteristics of firms that win design awards are fairly stable over time, yet paradoxically the firms that won awards in 1974 are not the main award winners in 1979 (the correlation between the two five-year measures of awards is only .40).

To understand why offices that survived won fewer or more awards in 1979 than in 1974 and also why award winning is not very stable, it is important to take into account the initial characteristics of firms and how they changed. Unlike the earlier analysis of the 1974 data on award winning, this longitudinal (indeed, panel) analysis permits genuine causal inferences because of the built-in time element.

The tendency to improve or decline in quality is primarily due to six factors.[13] The most important factor that contributes to an increase in awards is being large in 1974 (but growth in firm size has no consequence for an increase in awards). The next three factors that are roughly equivalent in their importance for improving quality are a gain in the diversity of client types over the five-year period, low productivity in 1974, and the tendency not to have used engineering consultants in 1974. Also firms that had employed a relatively large number of technicians in 1974 were less likely to win awards in 1979. Finally, the existence in 1974 of personnel rules significantly increased the likelihood of winning awards over the next five years, and although adopting such rules between 1974 and 1979 is also positively related to winning awards, it is not statistically significant. All things being constant, earlier award winning is unrelated to later award winning because firm size is largely responsible for both.

These findings confirm some of the results for the cross-sectional analysis in table 5.1. Size, contrary to professional lore, is a great asset for high quality, but a main feature of large firms is that they have a relatively small architectural staff and a large technical staff, both of which handicap their capacity to do good design work. This handicap becomes more pronounced with time. Using engineering consultants did not impair the work of firms in the earlier period, but such dependence is detrimental in the long run. As was evident in table 5.1, personnel regulations in 1974 are related to winning awards, but that was simply due to the fact that large firms had such regulations and also won awards. Yet over the long run personnel regulations become increasingly important for awards. Architects mentioned to me that having office personnel policies is consistent with merit because it increases the security of staff members, who know where they stand, and because it maintains high guidelines for recruitment. These are important considerations, apparently, in times of economic decline. Although we have seen that high productivity helped the eccentric small firm win awards in 1974 (and it had a slight negative effect among large firms), in the long run an emphasis on sheer output generally impairs quality, in support of architects' derision cast on the production firm (as against the design firm).

The details of this analysis are now cast in more general terms. There are three overall conclusions that together highlight a paradox of success: award winning slightly increases the likelihood of survival in a declining economy; the characteristics of firms that win awards in 1974 are similar to the characteristics of firms that win awards in 1979; most of the firms that win awards in 1979 are not the same as those that did in 1974. There are two plausible interpretations, with some truth in both. One interpretation that helps to account for the observation that different firms win awards in 1974 and in 1979 is that the standards of award juries change at a different pace than does the work of firms. The second interpretation takes into account the fact that a certain proportion of all the firms did continue to win awards, so that winning awards in 1979 can partly be explained by changes in firm conditions over the five-year period. Aside from small size the factors that make the greatest difference for a decline in quality are the following: an earlier emphasis on technical expertise, including engineering consultants and the reliance on in-house technicians, increasing productivity, and the failure to diversify client type. Tentatively I conclude that firms that have once established reputations for high-quality work did so on the basis of risk and high professionalism. The risks are incurred in a variety of ways: by small firms that venture eccentric structures and atypical practices; by articulating agendas and ideological climates, which in the small professionalized firm nurture high-quality work; by large offices that resist the tendency to rely on technicians to achieve savings and to protect their professional core. These forms of risk are discovered to foster merit, yet they are also financially costly, require a great deal of dedication, and in the long run are difficult to maintain. When organizational rationality takes over and routine procedures and technical standardization minimize the emphasis on riskiness, they simultaneously reduce the likelihood of attempting risky projects. Thus the very factors that promote organizational security are the ones that are the undoing of merit.

Happy Clients

The extent to which clients return (specifically, the percentage of all clients over a five-year period that commission at least a second project with the firm) and the tendency of clients to refer other clients (the percentage of all clients over a five-year period that come on recommendation) are quality indicators too. Clients are pleased for a variety of reasons, which range from the interpersonal (their relationships with the staff members of the firm) to the objective (such as special services the firm provides or the cost of the project). Architects who lack, in contrast with other professions, a monopoly on services, have not been timid in putting good client relations at the center of professional concerns. Nevertheless there is ambivalence on two counts about this general issue. First, although in the parlance of architects "happy client" refers to the paying client, there is some concern that user satisfaction should be the prime concern (see Perin 1970; Deasy 1974; Brolin 1976; Friedman 1975, 1983). Second, there is the dilemma of maintaining artistic control over the project and keeping the paying client pleased at the same time (Larson, Leon, and Bollick 1983).

Yet to the extent that clients return to the office or send over other clients indicates that the office has been successful in its promotional efforts and in meeting the clients' wishes. In contrast with awards, the size of the office makes no great difference for either returns or referrals; moreover client happiness is not cut of one cloth. The characteristics of offices that have high return rates are very different from those that have high referral rates.

Understandably most clients who commission more than one project are businesses or corporations, and therefore firms with high repeat rates have few private clients.[14] Neither older firms nor larger ones have especially high repeat rates. Yet it is noteworthy that one of the main predictors of this indication of client satisfaction is having many architects in charge of the project. Although it is widely believed that clients prefer to deal with only one individual, which may be true, apparently loyal clients also like to see many people sharing work as well as responsibility for their projects. Whether this form of team practice develops in response to clients' preferences or whether team practice is conducive to multiple commissions is hard to say, but the relationship persists under statistical controls. Most interesting perhaps is the finding that the lower the quality (as measured by awards), the higher the client repeat rate. At first I assumed that this may be due to the fact that firms with high repeat rates specialize in a particular project type, such as industrial buildings, which would explain why they receive few awards, but there is no evidence that this is the case.[15] My interpretation is that these business and corporate clients who do multiple commissions are primarily interested in lower costs that are part of the overall package. The wealthy corporate or business client that is interested in more than one unique statement will commission with a different firm each time. But the wealthy client interested in buildings as investments will find the most cost-efficient firm and continue to employ its services.

Variation in the client referral rate is explained by a very different set of factors that account for variation in client return rate, and indeed the correlation between the two is zero (−.03). Offices with high referral rates are neither particularly small nor large, nor do they have especially low- or high-quality projects.[16] Their main mark is that they have many private individuals as clients, which means that they specialize in residences.[17] The referral network therefore is comprised of upper-income individual families who can afford an architect-built house and who have friends who can also. In contrast businesses, corporations, and government apparently operate in less informal and more bureaucratic ways, relying on procedural application and competitive bidding.

Firms successful in tapping the informal networks of upperclass families have a relatively informal approach to practice as well. They tend to rely for hiring on personal contacts, recruiting through collegial networks rather than through professional schools or agencies. Finally, client referral is related to the firm's tendency to carry out many projects on a joint venture basis. This might be explained by the fact that joint ventures provide firms an economical substitute for keeping a full complement of professionals, and in fact, firms with high referral rates exhibit some tendency to employ part-time architects ($r = .19$).

High quality is a buffer against failure, with award-winning firms more likely to survive than firms that had not won awards. Firms that can boast satisfied clients, either as reflected in a high return or referral rate, were no more likely to survive than other firms; the relationship between survival and the return rate is $-.02$ and that between survival and referral rate .03.

Having satisfied clients, at least as measured by multiple commissions and becoming known through the grapevine, turns out to be a middling reflection of true success as a professional office. The results for multiple commissions tend to support the notion that the firm that becomes particularly dependent on a single cost-conscious client can easily begin to mirror that client and as a result lose its integrity as a design firm. Nor is either measure related to productivity.[18] All of this suggests that promotional efforts to achieve dependable clients or clients with friends are somewhat misplaced.

Conclusions

Regarding the issue of whether ideas or material conditions are prior in determining outcomes, the results described here suggest a complex interaction: valued objectives that are motivated by very specific ideas about architecture are realized when they are consistent with the conditions of firm practice. The logical and valid connection between ideas and firm structure is a major contingency of high-quality work. Yet that very structure on which ideas depend to have consequence is composed of the main conditions that disadvantage firms in the market economy. When the aesthetic of subjectivism, a main current of humanistic thought about built architecture, takes root in firms particularly disadvantaged with respect to the resources required to win awards—firms that are new, underbureaucratized, and lacking wealthy clients—the firm becomes unusually advantaged. Similarly, when the cashbox aesthetics of formalism takes root in firms particularly advantaged in their organizational conditions and markets, in firms that normally produce projects of merit, their advantage declines.[19] In this way the contingency of ideas on conditions of practice reveals a clear and even moral logic that at the same time is a logic of eccentricity.

The most pronounced features associated with award winning are those that accompany large size and notably those of bureaucratization and rationalization. But it is not the large firm that particularly benefits from its normally bureaucratized and rationalized characteristics; it is the eccentric small firm that does. The small numbers of such offices that risk an inappropriate mode of practice—out of character with the normal restrictions of small scale—are unusually capable of doing high-quality work.

Large offices quite naturally have the key features that are requisite for high-quality projects that only a minority of small offices are able to acquire. They offer clients a wide range of services, are incorporated, are productive, and have formal office procedures. Although excessive complexity and much reliance on technicians offset the advantages of large firms, they are structurally advantaged in other ways. Nevertheless they have all of the features that can corrupt standards for practice; when an emphasis on profits, client satisfaction, or the outmoded design aesthetic of formalism whittles into structures with such rationalized and bureaucratized features, structural advantages go amok.

For these reasons, it is neither the commercial nor the bureaucratic conditions of architectural practice that explain why some firms and not others do high-quality work. First, there is a dialectic between ideas and material conditions, and sometimes the ideas undo the structure that is requisite for top design. Hugh Hardy (quoted in Diamonstein 1980:85) says quite correctly, "To get itself made, architecture has to be commerce." The results reported here support that point of view, but they also suggest that if architects take it very seriously, it leads to their undoing. Second, quality is not uniformly affected by any given feature of practice. Whereas an office of a given size tends to have certain predictable characteristics owing to the sheer consistency of organizational dynamics, I find, particularly for small firms, that it is mainly when they violate those predictable and natural laws of organizational theory—that is, when they acquire characteristics they should not have—they are more likely to do outstanding work.

The paradox that early high quality contributes to survival chances but fails to contribute to continuing quality can be understood as part of the process of the routinization of firm practice. Engaging in innovative work is risky, especially in a declining economy. To routinize practice—specifically to rely increasingly on engineers and technicians—was the solution that most high-quality firms found to be the most satisfactory. This solution helped to save them from ruin, but it also led to work of mediocre merit.

There is no evidence to suggest that modern forms of patronage as evident in acquiring loyal clients promotes high-quality work, and in fact offices with many multiple commissioners tend to win few awards. This is consistent with the finding that firms that increased the diversity of their client types between 1974 and 1979 experienced substantial gains in the numbers of awards they won. And, because indicators of client satisfaction are unrelated to any success criterion (awards, increase in awards, productivity, and profits), I can conclude only that the significance of loyal clients for architecture is practically nil.

6

Dialectics of the Marketplace

Having an unlikely, indeed an eccentric, organizational structure offsets the disadvantages that the small practice has in competition for recognition of excellence; there is no evidence that the risks incurred by eccentric firms lead to their undoing. In general high-quality firms, small and large, eccentric and normally disadvantaged, were more likely to survive through the subsequent five turbulent years while lower-quality firms failed or left the city. Yet regardless of the fact that merit contributes to viability, merit does not contribute much to viable merit—continued award winning. Most surviving firms that were the top award winners in 1974 no longer were in 1979. There are two plausible explanations.

Taste and fashion have a dynamic of their own, and when architectural styles change, some firms do not change with them and get left behind. In the early 1970s the international style was clearly dominant, with only occasional experimentation, but there was also widespread disillusionment among rank-and-file architects. By the late 1970s marginal experimentation gave way to wide exploration of alternative styles. Under conditions of rapid change we can expect that the youthful firms with recent graduates who are skeptical of older models and have fresh ideas about design gain a competitive edge in design innovation. This is the case. Whereas older firms were more likely to win awards in the early 1970s, this was no longer true later.[1] When age or any other structural advantage is undercut by independent forces, such as changes in taste and fashion, we can consider this a disturbance of the status quo and a likely prelude of dialectical change. The second and more straightforward explanation for why firms could not keep up their meritorious track records is that the major preoccupation after 1974 was to get business, to stay alive. Concern with the marketplace and the architecture firm's hold on it dominated professional planning and office practice during this period.

The Economy

The effects of the nationwide recession that began in the early 1970s were most pronounced on construction in 1973 and then seriously affected architecture. There was a national decline of 12 percent of employment of architects between 1973 and 1976, with more than half of this decline occurring in late 1974 and early 1975 (American Institute of Architects 1975, 1977). But although building activity began to pick up across the nation by 1976 and even improved by 1978, the local economy in New York City hit a low bottom in 1976 as the result of the municipal fiscal crisis. New York City's poor economic conditions are indicated by a 10.4 percent overall unemployment rate in 1976, double what it had been in 1971, and well above the overall rate of 7.9 for all large metropolitan areas (U.S. Bureau of Labor Statistics 1973, 1975, 1976). Construction activity was dramatically down in the city, evidenced by a 33 percent drop in construction employment from 1974 to 1977 and a 14 percent decline in the same period in the number of construction establishments (U.S. Bureau of the Census 1974, 1976, 1977).[2]

This general decline in New York City created for organizations of all types an environment of uncertainty and the threat of business loss or ruin (Weinstein 1977). Some organizations were less dependent on the city and the resources it had to offer, and for many of them relocation was a reasonable option. But many organizations—architecture offices being a case in point—were too closely tied to this particular metropolitan environment, and staying in New York City after 1974 was a Hobson's choice; there was no alternative, but staying meant a high risk of failure.

Architecture firms that were initially attracted to the city were among the most prestigious design firms in the country. Manhattan is important for architects partly for symbolic reasons: it is the undisputed center for creative and artistic enterprise in the nation, if not the world. But also important are the special resources on which architecture firms depend: the many schools of design and architecture that provide recruits, specialized consulting firms located in the city, and a wealthy (and discriminating) clientele. Paul Goldberger (1975:43) wrote in an early lean year, "Somehow, in spite of the fact that building business is in a genuine depression in New York, none of the New York-based architecture firms seems to have given a thought to moving away. Many of them are doing their buildings elsewhere, of course . . . but this remains the city in which most architects want to be based." Goldberger's pronouncement was somewhat premature; many firms did not survive in the city.

I define failure as the inability of a firm to remain chiefly intact and to survive as an enterprise in New York City. For business enterprises in general the distinction between survival and failure is much less clear. As Kaufman (1976:27) points out, the line between healthy transformation and demise is difficult to draw when there is a merger, a corporate takeover, and even legal bankruptcy and reorganization. But professional organizations are not businesses in the same sense. Their integrity and distinctiveness are defined by a core staff of professionals and established traditions rather than in strictly financial terms. The personalized name of any architecture firm and its singular logo on the letterhead draw attention to what in fact makes it an integral organization. Thus surviving firms are those that remain intact, including those that became absorbed within a larger corporate structure or consortium (because this involves financial and legal changes, not more basic organizational and professional ones) and also those with relatively minor changes in the core staff.[3] Of the offices that failed, the vast majority disbanded, although a few may have moved away.[4]

The procedures used to identify survivors and failures included telephone calls and letters and consulting the state's professional registry and telephone directories. This search yielded ninety-two surviving firms, each of which was successfully contacted for an interview.

Death and Survival

Why Firms Fail
One explanation of why organizations fail is similar to the explanation of why any species of plant or animal becomes extinct: it is ill adapted for survival. The organizational ecology model draws from Darwinian functional theory by positing that organizations that are suited to their environment are least likely to

fail. In his comprehensive review of the theory, Aldrich (1979) states the main point:

The population ecology model, based on the natural selection of biological ecology, explains organizational change by examining the nature and distribution of resources in organizations' environments. Environmental pressures make competition for resources the central force in organizational activities. . . . Organizational *forms*—specific configuration of goals, boundaries, and activities—are the elements selected by environmental criteria, and change may occur through new forms eliminating old ones or through the modification of existing forms. (Pp. 27–28.)

In such a model organizational death is easily accounted for: "The first and purest form of environmental selection is the *selective survival or elimination of entire organizations*—organizations are either fit for their environment, or they fail" (Aldrich 1979:40; also see Hannan and Freeman 1977:939–940). On the basis of the model and even on commonsense grounds we should expect great differences among offices that managed to ride out the economic recession and those that could not. Such extraordinary economic forces that result in the ruin of 40 percent of a set of organizations are expected to operate in a systematic way, just as epidemics tend to take the lives of those least fit—the very young, the very old, the poor, the already ill.

We have learned that award winning does have some survival value.[5] But from what one understands to be the political economy of businesses, even professional ones, we expect that other factors play a more critical role in determining which firms survive. The most straightforward prediction from ecological theory is that offices buffered from the direct impact of the recession—through ties with large corporate clients, through their own initial political and economic advantages (a corporate organization, initial high productivity, initial high profits), or by successful exploitation of unique markets—are most likely to survive.

But contrary to this notion that there is systematic selection so that the fittest organizations survive, there are no characteristics that distinguish offices that managed to survive from offices that failed. That is, there is nothing to indicate that surviving firms compared with others had distinctive internal structures, that their clients were richer and more powerful, that they had special expertise and experience with particular types of projects, or that they had developed cost-effective ways of subcontracting or participating in joint ventures. Detailed features of firms—different ways of recruiting, office procedures, office technology, and specific client services—make no difference whatsoever for the chances of survival or failure. An extensive examination of firm characteristics that could possibly make a difference yielded only one: the few firms that had specialized in medical centers were slightly more handicapped than other offices. Yet this is fairly trivial and not theoretically important. Not even the characteristics of staff members from the 1974 survey (average age, nature of their professional training, percentage of architects who are registered, whether architects tend to be specialists or generalists) are different in a comparison of firms that failed by 1979 with firms that survived.[6]

These findings give the impression that organizational death is a random process. They indicate that failure and survival do not depend in any important way on any single characteristic of a firm or any combination of characteristics of a firm. But this seems highly implausible in a competitive capitalistic economy. Indeed refined analysis discloses that dividing firms merely on the basis of survival and failure oversimplifies the complex nature of possible organizational outcomes. The important distinction to make, and the one that can be empirically explained, takes into account the fact that some firms just barely survive, not quite going bankrupt but still teetering on the verge of it, whereas others do fail, and still others prosper in some respect or another. This is a fairly simple idea, though the process that underlies these divergent outcomes is complex.

Before describing this process, it is interesting to examine what strategies the heads of offices employed in coping with what they viewed as a crisis. The retrospective accounts provided by architects who headed firms that were still in New York City by 1979 provide ample evidence of rational and well-developed plans for coping with the new problems posed by the difficult economic environment. The efficacy of these plans is another question.

Firm Heads' Accounts

In the interviews carried out in 1979 principals were asked how the recession had affected their practice and several more specific questions about their strategies of dealing with the recession.

The vast majority, 62 percent, said that the recession had taken a serious toll on their offices. To be sure their accounts differ in detail; some offices had incurred high debts, others dissolved partnerships, and some moved into smaller quarters. Although it is impossible to quantify the nature of the dilemma that architects experienced, a common theme is the compromise of professional objectives: having to seek out commissions they would have scorned as pedestrian at an earlier time, seeking loans from relatives, working for clients whose politics or ideology they found objectionable.

Not all firms experienced such difficulties. About 20 percent of the principals with whom I talked said they had no serious cutbacks or loss of work after 1974, and nearly as many (18 percent) said that, if anything, they were better off by 1979. Generally the heads of firms who said that "things are going fine" could not identify the reason why: "good luck, I guess"; "knock on wood."

Specific strategies employed to cope with the recession are important to explore in order to find out whether they in fact worked. A reflexive response to a decline in commissions is to lay off staff, although this was reported to be a difficult decision. About half (53 percent) of the ninety-two surviving firms terminated some personnel; the first to go generally were technicians, engineers, and support staff. About one-third of the offices reorganized, which in nearly every case meant incorporation or becoming an affiliate of a corporate firm. Changes in leadership (for example, taking on a new partner or eliminating a vice-presidency) were reported by forty-one of the ninety-two principals; even without a base of comparison, this seems high.

Another calculated strategy was to identify and pursue new markets. For some firms this meant seeking foreign commissions; for some it meant identifying a different clientage than the office had had in the past; for others it meant diversification of projects and clients. About half (51 percent) mentioned this

as a prime objective when it appeared that traditional markets
were on the verge of collapsing.

As early as the 1960s there had been a growing interest among
architects in exploring ways of capitalizing on energy-efficient
technologies with design potential, from underground housing
to solar panels. In the 1970s there was a significant change in
official professional rhetoric; architecture was not a luxury, and
employing these new technologies in building practices could
cut costs (see, for example, Bailey 1975; Gutman 1977). Although most energy-saving technologies, architects told me,
were still too costly in the short run to be attractive to the average client, about 60 percent of the principals had incorporated
expertise in such technologies into their practices, with the an-
ticipation that this might be attractive to certain clients.

There also had been a growing interest in recycling structures
and renovation throughout the 1960s, but with the exception
of work on historical buildings, most established architecture
firms had little interest in such commissions, perceived to require more craft than art. In 1974 less than 10 percent of all
offices did any restoration or renovation work. By 1979 such
work had become the bread and butter for many firms that had
lost their other sources of income. Of the surviving firms 75
percent had begun to emphasize renovation within the last few
years.

In addition to asking each principal about layoffs, reorganization, renovation work, and so forth, I posed this follow-up
query: "What else did you do to cope with the recession?" The
answers to this question are only suggestive because the question was asked in such general terms. Some principals mentioned streamlining; for a few this meant more formalization
and better systems of accountability and for others doing away
with particular services.

Missing from my account of strategies of survival are the
emotions that accompanied their responses. It is not simply
a matter of maintaining a toehold in the market; economic
chaos, I was told in various ways, was no fair test of an architect's
mettle.

Efficacy of Strategies
Recent books written for architects by management specialists
have noted that architects are bound by traditional modes of
operation and fail to deal rationally and flexibly with modern

markets (see Bachner and Khusla 1977; G. Jones 1973; A. Wilson 1972). There is no evidence in this study to support that conclusion. Architects, though often desperate, carefully weighed a variety of alternative strategies, adopting some and ignoring others. It is assumed in both management science and some domains of sociology that organizational actors who act rationally in shaping the goals and objectives to meet environmental challenges can shape organizational outcomes (Peterson and Berger 1971; Zaltman, Duncan, and Holbeck 1973; Chandler 1962; Child 1972; Miles 1982). This is the assumption I now put to the test.

Changes in a firm's level of performance can be measured by comparing its standing on a performance criterion in 1974 with that in 1979. More precisely the relative gain (or loss) in performance is the difference in the level between 1979 and 1974, divided by the level in 1974. Thus we compare gains or losses relative to where the firms were at the beginning of the recession. There are multiple indicators of what can be considered superior performance: productivity (annual number of projects), merit record (award winning over a five-year period), profits (proportion of projects over a five-year period with construction costs exceeding $1 million), services (number of comprehensive services offered clients), diversity of clients (having many different types of clients rather than just a few),[7] professionalized staff (the proportion of all staff that are architects), securing new markets outside the city (proportion of all projects that are not commissioned for the New York City area), having dependable clients (client repeat rate), and size (total number of personnel). For these indicators of performance information is available for both 1974 and 1979, and relative change with respect to each of them was computed.

What strategies firm heads employed in attempting to ride out the recession or to turn the firm around make essentially no difference for what actually happened. Examining each of these nine performance measures and each of the strategies employed by architects, I find little evidence that strategies are effective.[8] In some instances strategies are counterproductive; firms in which there was a change in leadership underwent a relative loss of professional staff (with a corresponding increase in the percent technical and support staff); offices that identified new types of clients experienced relative declines in profits; offices that emphasized renovation suffered losses in profits and services. There is one exception to the generalization that strategies are without positive benefits: offices that began to emphasize energy-saving technology as a way of attracting new types of clients expanded the range of services they offered.

There may have been rare instances of inspirational leadership that resulted in profound recovery, but there is a notable absence of any evidence that a particular scheme or approach had systematic effects of pulling offices up by their bootstraps. These strategies may very well have helped to keep firms afloat, but they were remarkably unsuccessful in doing anything more than that.

There is an explanation for why some firms fail, others barely survive, and others even thrive, but it depends on more basic—structural—characteristics of offices than leadership decisions. The crucial principle is that certain practices are riskier than others, and these make both success and failure more likely. Although one can consider a wide array of indications of effectiveness, including the repeat rate and an expansion of services, there are only three that are important in the economy of firms, and all denude architecture of its professional trappings: size, profits, and productivity.

Fulcrum of Risk

If the first and second principles of organizations are survival and growth (Hodgkinson 1978:180–182), the third and fourth are productivity and profits. My approach is to combine the mark of ultimate success—simple survival—with relative change on each of the three other dimensions: size, productivity, and profits. Thus there are three sets of comparisons under consideration: a comparison of firms that failed with both firms that survived but whose profits did not increase or even decreased and firms that survived and whose profits increased; a comparison of firms that failed with those whose productivity stayed constant or declined as well as those whose productivity increased; and a comparison of firms that failed with firms that survived but did not grow and firms that expanded in size.[9] On the basis of the evidence presented thus far, survival or failure appears to be the result of mere luck. This, however, is decidedly not the case when we compare failure with relative success on one of these dimensions, for failure and success imply risk taking, which distinguishes both from sheer survival.

Failure and Profitability

Offices that merely survive are distinctively different from offices experiencing either a relative increase in profits or failure. Firms in the last two categories were remarkably similar in other respects in 1974. The most important characteristics they shared were small size and lack of affiliation, but they were also similar in that they had large numbers of projects outside the city, many referrals, many private clients, and a tendency not to use outside consultants. The diagrammatic summary of the results is shown in figure 6.1. As the figure indicates, failures were somewhat smaller (and less likely to be affiliated and so forth) as were those that flourished and became more profitable during the recession compared with those that survived, just maintaining a constant rate of profitability. These results spell out what the zone of safety can be in times of economic recession and also the factors of high risk, factors that tip firms to insolvency or to enrich them.[10]

To cast these results in more general terms, both failing and feathering the nest are likely outcomes for the independent entrepreneurial firms—ones that are small, autonomous, not tied to the local market, rely on dependable clients, use referral

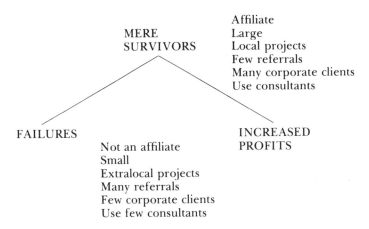

Figure 6.1
Summary of results for "failure," "profits stable or decline," and "profits increase"

networks, commission small projects for private clients, and depend on in-house staff rather than consultants. These are offices that have an inherent flexibility because they are not constrained by a cumbersome internal structure, by a parent corporate firm, or by dependency on construction activities in New York City. The absence of such constraints allows entrepreneurial firms to move quickly into increasingly profitable markets. But although these features are unconstraining, they are also risky. Small scale, the absence of protection that affiliation offers, and a reliance on projects far away from the office (as well as a dependence on referrals, small private clients, and the failure to use outside specialists) are special vulnerabilities. If entrepreneurial firms do not succeed in increasing their profits, they are unable to coast on low profit margins and hence fail.

What is fail-safe with respect to organizational death but not particularly advantageous with respect to improving profits is a set of features that define the highly rationalized office: large scale, corporate affiliation, local projects, an aversion to using client networks, reliance on primarily corporate and government clients, and the use of outside consultants. These features are buffers against organizational death and allow firms to weather the storm. On the other hand they do not enable firms to exploit new markets and thereby to advance their profitability.

Thus the fulcrum of risk in the case of failure and profitability depends on entrepreneurship. The flexibility of small offices is also their liability; they can tip either way. The established large firm, in contrast, is both unlikely to fail and unlikely to prosper.

Failure and Productivity
It is a common belief among architects that "some [offices] do a lot and others do it big" (see Larson, Leon, and Bollick 1983), which implies that some firms are very productive and turn out many small projects whereas others concentrate on a few but very expensive buildings. This is not true for these firms. In both the 1974 and 1979 surveys, productivity and profits are unrelated to one another; they are not negatively related.[11]

Although productivity is therefore a very different indicator of business success from profitability, it can be explained in comparable terms. In this analysis I juxtapose failure with no increases in productivity and productivity gains. Those that merely survived and did not experience increases in number of commissions over this period are the large, rationalized firms, ones that moreover had captured corporate markets. Although they offered relatively few client services, they designed more different types of projects than did other offices. These results are summarized in figure 6.2.[12] The mere survivors in this analysis of productivity change are similar in many respects to the mere survivors in the analysis of profit change. Firms that simply did a mediocre business—not a lot but enough—are firms that are the preeminent giants in the commerce of architecture. They were large, had predominantly corporate clientage, and had sufficient resources to work on many different types of projects at the same time. Such offices did not improve very much during the five-year recession but had sufficient resources to maintain a fairly steady work load.

In contrast, less established and less rationalized firms either bounded ahead to acquire a substantial increase in commissions or slipped backward and failed. Offices with few corporate clients, that were small, offered many client services, had not invested in a computer, and specialized in one or a few types of projects fall in one of the two extreme categories. Again we see that the fulcrum of risk in the case of failure and productivity affects most the small, entrepreneurial firm as it does in the case of failure and profitability. In contrast the mere survivors demonstrate a capacity to balance themselves, without having to incur risks yet without making great strides either.

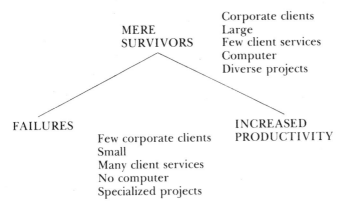

Figure 6.2
Summary of results for "failure," "productivity stable or decline," and "productivity increase"

Failure and Growth

An explanation of change and transformation is incomplete without examining growth. To expand during a recession indicates a remarkable capacity to cope when other firms cannot, to be unusually successful when competition is at its keenest. In this analysis, as in the previous ones, the combination of 1974 characteristics that defines a single function differentiates three groups of firms: failures, those that remained the same or declined in size, and those that increased in size.

The general features of firms that were high risk for increases in profits and increases in productivity are highly comparable. Small entrepreneurial offices in both cases are the ones most likely to be highly profitable or highly productive and the ones most likely to fail. What is risky for the chances of expansion and what is safe for the chances of keeping personnel more or less constant involves somewhat different factors than those involved in money making and sheer productivity. But the essential fact remains that those that thrive and those that fail are more alike than the intermediate firms that stay the course. As figure 6.3 shows, offices that grew between 1974 and 1979 initially were highly professionalized (that is, had a high percentage of architects on their staff), tended to specialize in one or a few projects, and had a large proportion of corporate clients. Firms with these characteristics were just as likely to fail too, indicating that this is a risky combination. Offices with a low percentage of architects on the staff, diversified projects, and few corporate clients were the ones that had a low growth potential but had developed immunities against failure.[13]

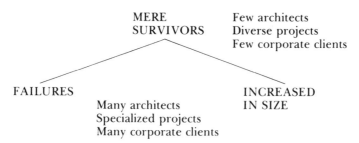

Figure 6.3
Summary of results for "failure," "size stable or decline," and "growth"

Reliance on corporate markets combined with a large, rationalized firm structure has not been found to be a liability, but this combination does not greatly contribute to productivity or to profitability. This is merely a fail-safe combination, protecting the firm from failure. Yet when reliance on corporate clients accompanies a strong professional orientation—one geared more to design than to production—the office incurs high risks. It will either thrive and expand or it will fail.

Why entrepreneurship is risky for firms in the middle of a recession is fairly clear. They can wheel and deal with greater flexibility than can the large firms tied to valued clients, yet they lack the built-in protections of large firms. The reason why the professionalized firm with corporate clients is a hazardous combination is because it is a contradiction to begin with. Most offices with a large architectural component do not work for corporate clients; moreover such professionalized offices tend to have relatively informal structures, with decentralization of decision making and few rules, which disadvantage them in high-powered markets.[14] When the unlikely happens—that is, when the highly professionalized firm secures corporate clientage—the contradiction is either resolved—which is most likely in a declining economy—through failure or turned to the firm's advantage. Such contradictions can vitalize an enterprise—if they are not lethal.

These fairly complex results for growth and commercial success can be summarized in a relatively simple way. By and large what is most critical in staving off disaster (but at the same time not ensuring spectacular gains either) is sufficient size and corporate commissions. In combination with other firm characteristics (such as computer technology and specialized client services), size and corporate clientage together provide immunities against failure, and there is little risk in that combination. On the other hand the design-oriented office that relies on corporate clients plays a "dicey" game; it has a chance to expand if it does not go bankrupt first. The design office is thus vitalized by corporate clients but at the same time rendered vulnerable by them.

Ordinary and Extraordinary Times

No one can predict for a single organization whether it will prosper, but social scientists have a good understanding of characteristics of organizations that generally promote a favorable outcome, that is, can predict with some degree of confidence top performance or middling success. Although the population ecology model is addressed primarily to the issue of survival, other theory and research focuses on effectiveness among viable organizations. Under ordinary conditions organizations that are most effective in meeting their commercial and other objectives have the following characteristics: they are relatively large (Starbuck 1965; Pfeffer 1972; Deeks 1976), have established diverse linkages with other organizations through affiliation, joint ventures, or consultancies (Osborn and Hunt 1974; Hirsch 1975; Evan 1971; Katz and Kahn 1966; Aiken and Hage 1968; Paulson 1974), have a complex internal structure and a diversity of products or services (J. Q. Wilson 1966; Hage and Aiken 1970), and have instituted formal routines and technologies to achieve coordination (P. M. Blau 1968; Perrow 1972).

In ordinary times organizations are naturally stratified, and the inequalities among them with respect to growth, profits, productivity, or any other indicator of effectiveness are due to these factors that tend to have uniform effects on performance. There is, in addition, another set of factors that operates more powerfully to give some firms not just relative advantage or disadvantage but appears to be so important that it bifurcates all organizations into an economic core of powerful and wealthy establishments and a periphery of marginal ones. Specifically organizations that are successful in establishing themselves beyond the uncertainties of entrepreneurship and into the corporate sector of the economy are absolutely advantaged (Averitt 1968; Braverman 1974; Clegg and Dunkerly 1980; Heydebrand 1983a).

Taking 1974 as a normal year for architectural offices, those features of offices that are expected to produce commercial benefits do in fact tend to have that effect. Productivity and profits in the prerecession period (I do not have information on growth before 1974) are positively and directly related to what are considered to be favorable structural conditions, such as large size, diverse linkages, internal complexity, diversity of products and services, formalization, and advanced technologies. And in 1974 firms with corporate clients and those that were themselves incorporated tended to be especially advantaged. Thus in ordinary times firms' success in economic markets can be explained in terms of models developed to understand effectiveness for any kind of organization.[15] In such times ordinary principles of organizations in a capitalistic economy apply to architecture firms just as they apply to any other type of business.

Dire straits, however, disrupt the normal processes by which firms get sorted in the economy. What under ordinary conditions create relative disadvantage, under extraordinary ones are conditions of risk, and what under ordinary conditions create absolute advantage, under extraordinary ones simply define a zone of safety. In terms of commercial outcomes features that are generally advantageous in normal times—notably large size and many corporate clients—in bad times become mere buffers against failure. And what is generally disadvantageous for business in normal times—features of entrepreneurship—become in bad times the conditions of high risk since they either allow the firm to maneuver quickly or engender demise. Whether firms grow, maintain a steady size, or fail depends on somewhat different characteristics from these, although because firms that grow and firms that fail are more alike than are firms that are stable, we can conclude that growth is governed by the same principle: a fulcrum of high risk. With respect to growth, having corporate clients is not a buffer against failure; rather it constitutes an element of high risk under the specific condition that the firm is highly professionalized.

Offices with a relatively large architectural staff are very unlikely to have many corporate clients, yet such offices can either capitalize on the high talent and high resource combination and continue to grow in spite of the economy, or they fail. Accommodation to corporate elites and the full realization of modes of practice forged from rationalized and technocratic elements is the direction in which highly professionalized organizations are bound (Heydebrand 1983b; Larson 1980), but in architecture this process is likely to be discontinuous and perhaps for that reason manifestly obscure. Because architecture is so intimately connected with the arts and is still organized to deal with traditional patrons who value good taste over efficiency, the foothold in impersonal corporate markets is tentative at best. Highly professionalized offices are contradictions to begin with, and a declining economy fully discloses the significance of such contradictions for practice.

Conclusions

The dialectics of change and transformation depend on contradictions between structures and their environments, in contrast to evolutionary processes that depend on compatibility
between structures and their environments. The assumption
behind the model of dialectical change is that what greatly advantages some social form—in this case, organizations—indeed, what is imperative for continued existence or growth, will
ultimately undermine that social form because of the accumulation of contradictions. In contrast the theory of evolutionary
change assumes that there is wide occurrence of variation in the
form and those particular features that are most adaptive or
most fit, will be retained.

In terms of sheer commercial success in 1974, there is fairly
strong evidence that architecture offices with the most adaptive
and most fit features, including being large and having secured
the most favorable commissions, were among the most successful in the economic competition for profits and output.
Their superior resources and their top performance in a stable
economy at first would imply their natural selection and continued vitality. They appeared to be functionally fit.

But this is not the case. The havoc created by the economic
recession totally disrupted any natural selection process that
may have been operating during normal times, and no type of
office or characteristic of office carried advantages for ultimate
survival. At the elementary level failure or survival during a
severe economic recession appears to be governed by a random
process; the sixty firms that failed differ in no important way
from the ninety-two firms that did not.

But a comparison between offices that closed and those that
did not is too crude, for it ignores the distinction between firms
that merely weathered the economic crisis and those that, in
spite of (or perhaps because of) the wide recession, found new
markets and new opportunities. Some offices increased the
scale of their projects and thus their overall profitability; others
increased the number of commissions, and others hired staff
and grew. Differences among these various outcomes can be
explained by the features of the offices—that is, by the types of
structures they had at the beginning of the recession, including
the way they were organized, their clients, and the nature
of their practice. In contrast, nothing that was deliberately

done—the calculated plans and strategies the principals report they employed during the period of the recession—makes the slightest difference for whether offices merely survive or whether they improve. Thus neither the theory of environmental selection nor the theory of administrative decision making can explain why the fates of offices are different from one another.

An explanation for demise, stasis, or success rests on the principle that normal advantages for growth and healthy commerce are contrary to the nature of a disordered and backsliding economy. The firms that were robust and had accommodated to markets in an expanding economy were partly undone by what had once been beneficial. Architectural firms that enfold and emulate the character of corporate capitalism, it can be concluded, are enfeebled when reliable markets begin to disintegrate. Nevertheless over a period of five years they were not utterly ruined but had merely retrenched; their initial resources provided them with a certain net of safety.

On the other hand, firms that exhibit the features of professional entrepreneurship have fates quite different from this. Though handicapped in normal times, they have the capacity to leapfrog and to overcome the once large and opulent firms. Failing this, they incur all the consequences of their initial vulnerabilities and go out of business. Whereas previously advantaged offices have features that are contrary to a declining economy, professional entrepreneurships have internal features that are contrary to one another and thus not well suited to a high-growth economy. Yet they are flexible enough to turn liabilities into assets in abnormal times. The outcomes of small entrepreneurial offices thus are explained as hinging on a fulcrum of high risk. Accordingly entirely different characteristics are adaptive in ordinary and in extraordinary times, and this is what produces the dialectics of historical development.

For one city, for a brief historical moment, we can capture the set of contradictions of contemporary architecture—as profession, as business. Dialectical processes of great consequence operate over much longer periods of time and affect many sectors of the economy. Nevertheless, a set of findings for a given set of organizations in a particular sector of the economy is generalizable, and the conclusions that can be drawn about the processes apply over longer periods of time and for other levels of analysis. For architecture in New York City it is fairly safe to conclude that as the local economy eventually improves, the large and more completely rationalized firms will again tend to dominate; but the dialectical process that turned their contradictions against them and generally upset the equilibrium allowed, if briefly, traditional entrepreneurship to appropriate design activities and architectural markets.

7

Architecture and the Daedalean Risk

There is an increasing awareness that advanced capitalism has gone haywire in building markets, which precludes the efficiency, the integrity, and the assumed morality of rational approaches to environmental design. This is significant at several levels. It means in urban design a disillusionment with systems theory and rational decision models. Theorist Manfredo Tafuri (1979:173) writes, "Indeed the present efforts to make equilibrium work, to connect crisis and development, technological revolution and radical changes of the organic composition of capital, are simply impossible. To aim at the pacific equilibration of the city and its territory is not an alternative solution, but merely an anachronism." The growing awareness that market mechanisms come into conflict with building and environmental design also entails the recognition that political potentialities underlie the aesthetics of architecture (see Fuller 1983), and they are more manifestly evident in its praxis. The politicization of the aesthetics of architecture is evident in the recent emphasis on buildings that appeal to a greater diversity of taste through their complexity, pluralism, and multiformity—that is, an architecture that gives expression to countervailing tastes, if not countervailing social and political interests (Jencks 1981; Hubbard 1980). The political potential of architecture is recognized by, among others, Friedman (1983), who would turn building over to the arena of direct democratic decision making. To be sure, architecture is not moving in one uniform direction, but what it is moving away from is clear: a model of rational equilibrium, purism, and functional orthodoxy.

On the whole social scientists too have jettisoned their models of equilibrium—the theories that posit functional integration—and now pay greater attention to understanding the sources of cleavages and dysfunctions in modern society. Current theoretical and empirical investigations focus on such issues as the ways in which advanced countries achieve dominance and keep other countries economically and militarily dependent, the segmentation in labor markets that reinforces initial differences in training and rewards between blacks and whites and between women and men, the confounding of class and minority status that produces a seemingly intractable source of inequality, and the concentration of capital and power in the monopolistic sector of the economy at the expense of the competitive, entrepreneurial periphery.

Not only do these forms of cleft structure rest on contradictions in society, they generate new antagonisms over time — for example, when women make gains in improving their educational qualifications only to find their degrees are worth less than men's and that the division of household labor is not significantly altered either.

Contradictions in professional practice have been the subject of this book. Although architecture alone was used to make the argument, and thus the forms the contradictions take are more or less specific to architecture, I assume that the underlying processes are generalizable. In chapter 1 I pointed out the features that architecture shares with other established professions. But it is also important to remember the ways in which architecture differs from them.

With the exception of engineering, architecture is more fully involved with technocratic and corporate elites than other professions, which creates unusual difficulties. One is ethical; a worthwhile objective in any profession is that it provide services to all clients, not just to the very rich and powerful. A second difficulty of its dependence on elites in the private sector is that architecture enjoys few of the legal and monopolistic protections accorded, for example, the health professioins, which are closely bound to public and quasi-public sectors. Moreover architecture's commercial standing is not very secure since it must compete with a large and efficient building industry to capture a corner of the market.

Whereas most other professional fields depend on a given theory that changes relatively slowly (the theory of genetic transmission, learning theory, or Newtonian physics, which suffices for most engineering fields), architecture (not unlike art and psychiatry, however) undergoes frequent apostasies as conceptions about design, function, and scale are routinely re-evaluated. Not all members of the profession are equally affected by this process of reevaluation and change in theory, but its consequences for practice are far-reaching. To mention just a few aspects of change: buildings can be outdated before they are completed; the possibility of introducing a new approach is open to anyone; one problem typically has many design solutions; and the relation between design theory and technological means is highly variable. Such flux implied by these uncertainties is an important reason why members of the profession are not closely integrated and often unable to act in concert on major issues facing the field.

Architecture is also far from uniform with respect to its educational and certification standards. In part this is because of different emphases placed on the various roles of the occupation: artist, business expert, bureaucrat, social reformer, user advocate, technician. One role, artist, is conceived to lie somewhere beyond the educational and credentialing process.

Finally, the integral importance of architecture to the public is far less than that of medicine and law. Medicine stakes its legitimacy on life and health, law on personal legal protection and public safety. Architecture has no comparable domains; in fact it cannot even lay exclusive claims on building, except on its design or artistic value inasmuch as most building is done without any architects. (To paraphrase Gropius, after engineers have finished the building, architects may be called in too.)

These features combine to make architecture a profession that is less organized than most others and relatively weak. Yet they also contribute to a greater vitality and openness, the lack of which makes most prestigious occupational groups opaque to outsiders. Controversies are widely aired, there is considerable variation in forms of practice, and individuals differ in the degree to which they adopt one or a combination of occupational models. From one angle this means there is ample range for addressing a number of questions of sociological interest.

In the remainder of this chapter, I review the main conclusions of this study from a perspective that emphasizes that these and other contradictions are important for they are responsible for change and transformation in the profession and practice of architecture. Social and economic structure figures predominantly in this process, but ideas play more than a casual role.

Ideas and Style

The question concerning the linkages among societal conditions, ideas, and architectural style is complex but can be addressed by the findings of this study. A brief summary of the contrast between architecture in premodern times and in contemporary societies helps clarify the issues.

In traditional Western and Oriental societies the values of the ruling class were easily translated into secular or religious buildings, as "architects appeared to mediate the 'affinity' between elites and stylistic conventions" (Larson 1983:53), and in relatively homogeneous cultures, without elites (and without architects), vernacular buildings reflected a "community of experience" (Rudofsky 1964). Such a close relationship between societal conditions and architecture, however, is undermined and often completely breaks down in contemporary Western societies.

There are three main explanations for why buildings appear now to be outside their historical times. One hinges on the assumption that social conditions govern or stimulate artistic ideas, which in turn find expression in building style. Although this chain of influence is clear enough, the process can be slow, in which case built architecture lags behind historical circumstances, or ideas may be reactive, in which case built architecture represents opposition to its historical circumstances. The second explanation assumes that architectural ideology is independent of circumstances and thus can engender changes in buildings with results independent of and unrelated to its context. The third explanation is that architectural products are not congruent with their times because they are capriciously influenced by social and economic conditions that are themselves in contention and flux; ideology may provide justification for architecture, but ideas themselves have no consequence.

To provide a concrete example, it is of interest to architectural historians that Beaux Arts' impractical romanticism took such deep roots in the later part of the nineteenth century, just at the time, Saint (1983:80) notes, that the "unsentimental priorities of capitalism were starting to gnaw at the cities." One view is that the Beaux Arts style was a reaction against commercialism and the rationality of capitalism (Richards 1970:36) while the international style represents acquiescence to it (Condit 1964). Ideology is thus not trivial, but it is more controlled by conditions than controlling them. The second explanation provided is that ideas about design respond, sympathetically or antithetically, to prior styles. In this vein Jordy (1976:349) argues that the Beaux Arts style was a reaction against the more naturalistic conceptions that had conditioned design in the earlier part of the century. Thus architectural intentions, not socioeconomic conditions, are the driving forces resulting in change. The third explanation of why buildings do not correspond to prevailing conditions is that architecture is controlled by contradictory and seemingly irrational, material forces in society (Colbert 1966; Tafuri 1980). To put the question in its most elementary form, Is architectural style largely the translation of ideas that respond to an objective reality; is it the product of ideas that themselves are autonomous; or is it driven by material conditions and beyond ideology?

What this study can lend to the controversy comes in the way of some empirical data, information obtained from architects and the heads of firms. I find that the ideas of rank-and-file architects are at fundamental odds with the prevailing style of built architecture and with the objectives evident in practice. That is, their ideas are altogether contrary to the monumentalism and stylistic poverty of the late versions of modernism and do not mesh either with the pragmatic priorities that govern the practice of architecture, at least as these priorities are stated by principals. The responses of architects may imply that they interpret the international style as the symbolic embodiment of monopoly capitalism and commercial imperatives and in its stead argue for an architecture based on humanistic values, for buildings that are less pretentious and more informal. In the absence of the organizational and economic constraints with which firm heads must contend, rank-and-file architects pay little heed to the interests of the paying client and say they would like to be more concerned with the users of buildings. It was only at the end of the 1970s that these revisionist ideas were clearly articulated by architectural critics and slowly and timorously incorporated into built architecture. This might suggest that a genuine avant-garde—one in full accord with its accomplished ideas—is impossible in architecture, and it might also suggest that ideas are not autonomously achieved or very effectual. These conclusions are not quite correct for they ignore the momentum required for new ideas to be consequential.

Initially social and economic conditions and the nature of organized practice impede the realization of new design conceptions. Yet something of a snowballing process takes over as ideas become organized, as critics articulate and thereby strengthen these ideas, and as experimentation occurs.

The analysis of the ideas of the firm heads—I call them agendas—clarifies the role of ideas in this process of change. The agendas that principals have about practice are found to be efficacious, but only provided that they are logically related to particular conditions of practice. The conditions to which agendas must be logically related to be effective are in fundamental opposition to other conditions; ideas themselves are inert, and although structural affinities give them potential power, it is the simultaneity of structural alternatives that empowers ideas. If an agenda of aesthetics is emphasized, it will be translated into quality, but only if the firm is small, highly professionalized, and nonbureaucratic. An agenda of profitability is not inherently inconsistent with attaining quality design, but it is inconsistent with it if the office is structured along the lines of an efficient, bureaucratic enterprise. Agendas, in short, must take root in appropriate social forms if they are to be potent and operative.

Yet the contrarieties of social forms themselves are just as important. That is, elements that make up unusual forms to provide the fertile soil for ideas to become translated into practice are themselves contradictory. They are in the sense that they represent combinations of firm characteristics that are atypical and anomalous themselves, and especially so for the production of merited buildings. For instance, the small professionalized firm faces deficits in staff support and marketing services and lacks the capability of doing large-scale work. It exhibits, in other words, features antithetical to those of well-established practices that quite naturally produce high-quality work. Even so, an achieved coupling between values of excellence and the features of the small professionalized firm is realized in recognition for merit, whereas it is not so realized in well-established forms of practice, which are otherwise normally advantaged in competition for recognition.

Ideas appear thus to play a role in affecting change, but they must be sown at the right time and the right place, which is to say a time and place of contrast or of contradiction with prevailing institutional forces. A well-documented historical example from the visual arts helps to substantiate this conclusion. Antal (1966), among others, has documented how the progressivism and humanistic ideologies of pre-Revolutionary French artists, of whom Jacques-Louis David is the most prominent example, became increasingly regressive as they continued to cater to bourgeois taste. They served, in fact, the very nationalism and elitism that courtly art had fostered for the ancien régime, an art against which they had ostensibly rebelled. It was not until the traditionally powerful Academy of Fine Arts began to collapse, in part by its own antiquated structure and in part by increasing competition from dealers, that ideological and stylistic revolt became possible (White and White 1965). But if it had not been for the ideas nurtured from the times prior to the Revolution and then sustained by Gericault and Courbet, the impressionists would not have been ideologically prepared to exploit the opportunities created by institutional contradictions.

The broad conclusion is that ideas have ontological status, yet paradoxically they are powerful when they are logically validated through being consistent with social structures that are themselves composed of antagonistic, or incompatible, elements. In other words, institutionally discordant conditions provide ideas with a greater chance to flourish and to be operative than they have under uniform and stable conditions. However, particular antagonistic elements must themselves be compatible with ideas; otherwise they would be mere pipe dreams or mere ideology in the original sense in the theory of historical materialism. Certain contrasting forms of organization empower the agendas of firm heads to be transformed into practice. In a broader historical context the polarities of institutional arrangements in France similarly created opportunities for painters. As for the convictions of rank-and-file architects, there is fairly good indication that progressive conceptions of design have acquired critical and public support through the snowballing process. Many chinks in the configuration of architecture production make it likely that with the accumulation of contradictory circumstances, dramatic changes can occur too in design practice that would make buildings more consistent with architects' convictions.

Architecture and Professionalism

Small and incompletely rationalized offices, though handicapped by diseconomies of scale, are the seedbed of ideas that produce high-quality work. And when they venture beyond the limits of their scale and flaunt their diseconomies, they do exceptionally good work. A complex structure, a large technical component, and bureaucratic formalization contribute to the likelihood of winning awards among smaller firms, in which these characteristics are least likely to be found. In contrast large firms usually have all of these features, and for that reason are normally advantaged.

The explanation for why small, peculiar firms excel is that eccentric surroundings are a spur to innovation. It appears that these firms retain many of the features of the small professional office while they undergo rationalization and bureaucratization at an uneven rate. For example, they have relatively open communication and a broad definition of employees' responsibilities, and they nurture a feeling of collegial camaraderie, while at the same time they are acquiring the organizational resources to obtain good clients and go after venturesome commissions. Firms that dare to take risks, act in a brazen manner in the marketplace, and at the same time preserve a congenial climate for the staff are often successful in closing the rift between professionalism and entrepreneurship.

Yet these are firms with internal contradictions. Over a five-year time span, the evidence suggests, meritorious offices with eccentric structures take the following trajectory: they usually survive as they become large and more completely rationalized (though sometimes they fail as they overextend themselves in the market). Thus what makes eccentric firms more likely to survive is their evolution in the direction of large, normally advantaged firms. In this way the risks they incur by their internal contradictions lead them to increasing normalization, at the cost that this undercuts their capabilities of continuing meritorious work. This is but one instance of the Daedalean risk.

Architecture and Bureaucracy

For the reason that architecture requires mastery of techniques and a complex technology and because its practice is also a business, the organization of architecture is accompanied by bureaucratic features. The main hallmark of bureaucratic organization is differentiation, not only of individuals in terms of specialties and jobs but also of groups of individuals by hierarchical levels, departments, teams, and work groups. Coordination is achieved through written procedures, operating rules, hierarchy, and an administrative staff.

Architecture requires a bureaucracy to which it is, in part, discrepant. For example, there are incongruities between the expectations of those who become architects and the restraints bureaucracy imposes on them. The notions of the creative genius and of architecture as high art are preserved and reinforced in many quarters, not only by professional schools but also by architectural historians and by critics.

Imagination, however, is not long left unfettered in the places of organized practice. I discovered a vast gap between architects' expectations about what their careers would offer—the chance to be creative—and the realities of organized practice—specialization, banal assignments, inequalities in voice, and few opportunities to have design responsibilities.

Another contradiction arises from a combination of one usual and one unusual circumstance. There is, first, the usual and inevitable specialization of individuals that accompanies large size, and there is, second, an unusual tendency of large firms not to have specialized practices. For both economic and organizational reasons, a large organization of any kind has more minute internal specialization than a small one. This means that people have specialized responsibilities and that the organization itself is divided into many specialized subdivisions. This is true for architecture firms as well. Unlike other enterprises, however, larger architecture firms are more generalist in character than small ones with respect to the kinds of activities in which they engage and the kinds of buildings they produce. The large firms in this study are much less specialized on major dimensions than small ones. They offer a wider array of client services, including, for example, mortgage services, landscape design, and prefabrication, and they work on more diversified project types (although they do not have a wider range of clients than smaller offices). In all other professions the emblem of a complex base of knowledge is specialization and narrow expertise; there is a strong push among law firms, medical and dental group practices, accounting offices, veterinarian clinics, and brokerage houses to reduce their scope of services (while, presumably, improving their quality). Architecture, on the other hand, remains wedded to the traditions of the liberal professions and has tended to resist such specialization, at least at the level of the organization.

The wide range of services and projects that the larger office undertakes affects the work of all of its individual members, and their involvement in diverse services and projects is translated into greater personal power. Nevertheless the extensive specialization with respect to project responsibilities in the larger office results in less personal power. To illustrate, an architect who works in a large eclectic practice has greater knowledge about many kinds of projects compared with the architect who works in a small office, but he or she is assigned narrowly circumscribed tasks—for example, financial analysis or specification development. This coupling of eclectic organizational practice with respect to services and projects with specialization of individual tasks has contradictory effects on individual voice in the affairs of the firm. The first tends to widen the opportunity for exercising voice, whereas the second tends to reduce it. Because the negative effects of individual specialization on power are far greater than the positive effects of firm comprehensiveness, architects employed in larger offices tend to have less power than those employed in smaller offices.

These findings help to sharpen our understanding of why architects disparage, in whatever vague terms, the big production firm, and additional findings further clarify the issues involved. The data show that the reduced commitment to work and the relatively weaker professional identification usually found in large firms are the result of the way in which jobs are structured in them and the lesser voice in the large firms' affairs that its architects have.

What mainly underlies high commitment is a wide scope of responsibilities and voice in organizational matters and the autonomy that such voice implies. Both are more likely to be found in smaller offices, although occasionally they are also found in specially structured large ones—those with relatively independent project teams rather than a departmentalized organization. It should be emphasized again that large firms are advantaged in multiple ways, in spite of their lower levels of participation and of morale. In ordinary times their advantages—high-quality work, high profitability—are not affected by liabilities of low morale. In extraordinary times they grapple

most with the dilemmas involving bureaucracy and professionalism, and architecture and business.

Illusionary Myths

"Architects were not meant to design together; it's either all his
work or mine."[1] Only the solipsistic conventions in architecture
make such a statement comprehensible. This romantic conception of the designer-artist, still a current of thought in contemporary architecture, is strikingly at odds with what I find to be
the basis of career commitment and vitality of architects' professional identity: voice and shared responsibilities.

Yet this is but one instance that traditionally rooted beliefs are
at variance with organizational realities. Another finding contrary to this romanticization of the individual in architecture is
that the more participatory the office, the more effective and
efficient it is as an organization and as a business enterprise.
Moreover, the democratically organized office is also most likely
to design projects of superior merit.

Still another conception that is found to have little empirical
support concerns the beliefs about clientage. It is often stated
that having loyal clients is a mark of professional success. Also,
having them, it is thought, makes it possible to dispense with the
unsavory business of marketing one's wares. Loyal clients, my
data indicate, have no clear benefits for practice, and they can
be risky in times of an economic recession. Correspondingly a
strong client orientation in the firm—that is, client satisfaction is
a main component of the organizational agenda—will reduce
the quality of the firm's projects when accompanied with a
bureaucratized practice.

Architecture and Business

In times of prosperity and growth, the commensuality between
corporate capitalism and architecture is clearly evident. Under
such conditions normally advantaged firms—those that are
large, corporate, and fully rationalized as organizational en-
tities—dominate core markets, markets that are highly organized and profitable. At the same time it is apparent that they
sow many seeds that potentially enfeeble them. Even before a
serious economic recession, their capacities as bureaucratic or-

ganizations begin to undermine their base of professionalism: departmentalization, a decline in the professional component and the routinization of work, a reduction in staff participation in decisions, and the consequent creation of social conditions that are not congenial to ideological progressivism. Most firms like these did survive the economic recession, but just barely; small entrepreneurial firms with a more intact professional focus tended to surpass them—and surpass them on their own terms, in productivity and profitability. The logic of the relative decline of the erstwhile core firms—modern offices integrated in corporate markets—is part of the dialectic of professionalism and commerce.

Another phase of the dialectic process is discernable when the contradiction between professionalism and commerce is resolved, even though the resolution is illusory. Some firms internally retain the contradictory features of high professionalism and successful integration in corporate markets. Yet they are more likely to fail than remain stable, just as they are more likely to expand and grow than remain stable. As such internalized contradictions are the very substance of dialectical transformation, it is to be assumed they are the immature predecessors of more completely rationalized offices that in time sheer off much of what becomes uncommon professionalism in big business.

The paradox is that firms that are likely to surpass the highly established and previously successful firms are those that are more subject to bankruptcy or ruin. They are governed by a potent structure of risk that contains within it the possibility of failure or great success. This is the principle of the Daedalean risk, and I have described the fates of the small professional firms as being suspended on a fulcrum: they cannot stand still for they lack the resources of the large, core firms to do so, and unless they seize the opportunities and thereby surpass core firms, they fail. Thus the dialectic of change in the practice of architecture can be seen from one perspective as the replacement of particular types of firms by others, but it also can be viewed as both resolution and creation of a series of contradictions over time. Economic forces that govern successful enterprise are counter to other forces that make architecture a successful profession, and this is what creates a dynamic of change and transformation.

Matter of Choice

An attempt was made here to consider the processes that affect a segment of the urban market, composed of a set of professional architecture firms and the architects who work in these firms. A series of contradictions were identified from the data analyses from which inferences were derived concerning dialectic change and principles that explain such change. These principles are summarized as follows: when two opposing conditions are internalized in a structure, one asserts itself over the other, and which does depends primarily on the prevailing economic climate; the economic forces that pull firms into the orbit of successful enterprise are counter to the forces of professionalism; yet the forces that pull firms into that orbit are weakened during economic recessions, creating opportunities for small, professional firms; although ideas do not in and of themselves instigate change, when they are logically connected with structured elements that themselves are in antagonistic relations with other elements, ideas help to precipitate change and establish the substance of the newly emergent forms.

Clearly implicit in these principles is that there are no predetermined outcomes. The piling up of contradictions is redolent with vast indeterminacy, which in turn creates the opportunities for experimentation and innovation. This conclusion is itself the logic of Marx's conception of the dialectic process. There is, moreover, another reason for expecting choice to matter, and this fortifies the first. Ideas are found to play a role in change, and although it is a conditional role, they are instrumental just at the point of potential impasse, specifically in the midst of structural contradictions. It can be said that although architecture—as profession, as theory, as practice— faces now fulsome predicaments, its future is in no sense a forgone conclusion.

Appendix: List of 1974 Firms

Ames, Kagan & Stuart
Avalone & Degenhardt
Welton Becket & Assoc.
Richard M. Bellamy
William Berg
Beyer, Blinder & Belle
William Breger Assoc.
Blythe S. Brewster
Brown, Lawford & Forbes
Harold Buttrick
Walker O. Cain & Assoc.
J. Gordon Carr & Assoc.
Augusto M. Camacho
Carson, Lundin & Thorson
Castro-Blanco
Caudill, Rowlett & Scott
Ayla Karacabey Chatfield
Russell C. Childs
George W. Clark Assoc.
Jack P. Coble
Coffey, Levine, & Blumberg
Earl B. Combs
Conklin and Rossant
Copelin & Lee
Cowell, Radenhausen & Geffert
Donald Cromley
Curtis & Davis
J. A. Daidone Assoc.
William J. Deardon
Richard B. Dempsey

Samuel J. DeSanto
Roy Euker
Evans, Delehanty & O'Brien
Feingersch & Prowler
Josh Feingold
Feldman, Misthopoulos Assoc.
Ferrenz & Taylor
Charles B. Ferris
Freidin, Kleiman Assoc.
Gina, Levi, Treffeisen, Architects
Horace Ginsbern & Assoc.
Myron Goldfinger
Leslie Malcolm Good
Miles A. Gordon
Henry George Greene & Assoc.
Victor Gruen Assoc.
Gruzen & Partners
San Anson Haffey
Leon J. Haft
Hagmann & Stern
Haines, Lundbert & Waehler
Halsey, McCormick & Helmer
Handren, Sharp & Assoc.
Hardy, Holzman, Pfeiffer Assoc.
Hausman & Rosenberg
Heery & Heery
David Paul Helpern Assoc.
Hoberman & Wasserman
Hurley & Farinella
Raymond Irrera Assoc.
Stephen Jacobs & Associates
Harley M. Jones
Kahn, Jacobs & Kaplan
Robert W. Kahn
Kallmann, McKinnell, Russo & Sonder
Kaminsky & Shiffer
Gerhard E. Karplus
Katz, Waisman, Weber, Strauss
Katzman, Kloke & Assoc.
Kennerly, Slomanson & Smith
S. J. Kessler & Sons
Milton F. Kirchman

Klein & Kolbe
R. M. Kliment
Richard Korchien (Environetics)
Nobuo Kusumi
Morris Lapidus Assoc.
Henri LeGendre & Assoc.
Stephen Lepp & Assoc.
Liebman & Liebman & Assoc.
Liebowitz, Bodouva & Assoc.
Liebriech
Arthur Lilien
Charles Luckman Assoc.
Thomas W. McHugh
Herbert L. Mandel
Marlo-Dechiara Associates
George J. Masumian
Richard Meier & Assoc.
Metcalf & Associates
Meyers, D'Aleo, Preiss & Barie
Mitchell-Giurgola Assoc.
Richard R. Moger
Mauro E. Mujico
George Nemeny
Martin Nystrom
O'Connor & Kilham
Julius Panero
Steven Papadatos
I. M. Pei & Partners
Carl J. Petrilli
Platt, Wyckoff & Coles, Architects
Pokorny & Pertz
James Stewart Polshek Assoc.
Lee Harris Pomeroy
Poor & Swanke & Partners
Potters & Williams
Prentice, Chan & Ohlhausen
Pritchard-Swan Assoc.
Carl Purchall Assoc.
Joseph Raggio
Donald Reiman
Manford H. Riedel
Norman Rosenfeld

Abraham Rothenberg
Robert L. Rotner
Paul Rudolph
William R. Sachs
Saffran & Hepperle & Assoc.
Claude Samton & Assoc.
Alan Sayles
Lee Schoen
Joseph B. Schwartz
Daniel Schwartzman
Gilbert L. Seltzer
Sharon-Krob-Murray
Shreve, Lamb & Harmon
Barry Silberstang
Skidmore, Owings & Merrill
Slingerland Architects
Richard W. Snibbe
Richard G. Stein
Walter Knight Sturges
Syrop & Rassic Assoc.
William B. Tabler
Edgar Tafel
David Todd & Assoc.
Vito J. Tricarico
L. E. Tuckett & Thompson
Emanuel L. Turano
Twitchell & Miao
Max O. Urbahn Assoc.
Urs-Hewitt-Royer
Van Summern & Weigold
Kenneth Walker Design Group
Warner, Burns, Toan & Lunde Assoc.
Maurice Wasserman
Max Wechsler & Assoc.
Weiss, Whelan, Edelbaum, Webster
Steven Winter
Maurice Wolff
Nakita Zukov

Notes

Chapter 1

1. Only about one out of every ten houses constructed in the United States involves an architect (Gutman 1983), although this is closer to about one-quarter for nonresidences (Saint 1983).

2. There are actually 745 listings under "Architects" in the 1974 Manhattan telephone directory, but 205 of these are the names of individual architects who are partners or leading designers in firms.

3. Why domes (and other structures) stand up is lucidly explained by Salvadori (1980).

4. Although it is true that statements derived from experiments are theoretically superior to probabilistic statements derived from statistical analyses, unless the ideal conditions can be approximated or unless it is possible to enumerate and measure most of the important disturbing influences, it is preferable to formulate causal statements in statistical terms so that the assumptions about error can be made explicit.

5. Some of the analyses reported are based on panel data, which are collected at two points in time. This portion of the study resembles a natural experiment, and the inferences derived from these sets of results are more powerful in dealing with the matter of causality than those based on cross-sectional data.

Chapter 2

1. One argument is that the state mirrors the economy because the state and economic enterprise work closely together for the protection of investment decisions. The assumption that powerful economic organizations alter state bureaucracy in this way is made by Karpik (1978). Another approach is based on the assumption that technocracy and neocorporatism are generic to all organizations and transcend the differences between public and private organizations and between service and product-making organizations (Heydebrand 1981). A final argument is Alan Wolfe's (1977). The state initially adopted as an objective the protection of private capitalism but then, facing a crisis of legitimacy, also adopted the objective of social welfare. The con-

tradiction between the two escalated the level of bureaucratization, without, he adds, contributing much to further either objective.

2. See the following for critical summaries of the consequences of Taylorism: Abrahamsson (1977), Hill (1981), Clegg and Dunkerley (1980:82–98). Earlier works provide a more positive treatment of the subject; examples are Drucker (1954) and Massic (1965).

3. For discussions concerning evidence of past and continuing discrimination in the profession against minorities and women, see Osman (1974), Kron (1980), Larson (1983), Huxtable (1974), Goldberger (1974), W. Gordon (n.d.).

4. Under present New York State laws, a newly incorporated architecture firm must be chartered as a professional corporation. It differs from a public corporation in that only licensed professionals can buy stock and the corporation itself cannot own stock in another company; like the public corporation, though, the professional corporation can invest profits. These firms are considered as corporations in the analysis and are distinguished from firms owned by a single architect or partners. Also included in the incorporated category are older firms that are still chartered as business corporations.

5. Some, little, and no influence are scored 3, 2, and 1, respectively. An average is not ideal because concentration in the hands of one individual theoretically can yield the same score as a situation in which all hold approximately the same power. The distribution of the standard deviations indicates this is not a problem, however. Moreover, the high consistency of results obtained using individuals as the unit of analysis and firms as the unit, combined with the advantages for interpretation of the mean compared with, for example, the standard deviation or the unstandardized slope, indicates that the mean is a superior measure for the purposes here.

6. The total list of tasks is: office management, job getting, financial development, feasibility studies, financial analysis, project analysis, programming, client relations, schematic design, design development, coordinating consultants, estimating, working drawings, writing specifications, bidding and negotiations, model building, graphic design, survey and site evaluation, land use studies, layout, construction administration, construction management, and real estate development.

7. The sixteen special services are feasibility studies, project analysis, financial analysis, programming, land use studies, construction management, interior design, industrial layout, innovative construction techniques, altering and remodeling, restoration and preservation, real estate investment, research, mortgage service, and two "other" categories. They are contrasted by the American Institute of Architects (n.d.) with the basic services offered clients. Virtually all firms offer the full complement of basic services.

8. More specifically, it is the number of full-time equivalent staff. Unless dichotomized, size is always transformed logarithmically (to base 10), to correct the highly skewed distribution of size.

9. Respondents were asked whether the firm had written policies governing the following: schematic design, detailing, estimating, specification writing, bidding and negotiation, and construction administration.

10. Technicians include primarily drafting personnel, estimators, specification writers, and others who do not carry out architectural responsibilities.

11. This is a combined total of the percentage of projects for which any of the following are consulted: structural engineers, mechanical engineers, and electrical engineers.

12. Each factor's simple correlation with the score of collective voice is reported here, with the partial correlation (controlling size) in parentheses: rules, $-.20$ (.03); age, $-.23$ (.02); technicians, $-.38$ ($-.06$); corporate status, $-.28$ ($-.01$); affiliate, $-.10$ (.14); engineering consultants, $-.26$ ($-.09$). The N is 100, the number of cases for which there is no missing data for the dependent variable, the power score.

13. This example is often used to illustrate spuriousness. To my knowledge, Paul Lazarsfeld (1955) was the first to employ it.

14. This is a path analysis. Reported in the following sequence are: the labeled connection; the variables in the causal sequence; the value of the path coefficient, p, and its level of significance as 1.5 (*), or 3 (***) times its standard error.

(A) Log size, Collective Voice, $-.39$***
(C) Log size, Firm's Task Complexity, .51***
(B) Log size, Individual's Task Complexity, $-.54$***
(E) Firm's Task Complexity, Collective Voice, .14*
(F) Individual's Task Complexity, Collective Voice, .42***
(D) Firm's Task Complexity, Individual's Task Complexity, .19*

The adjusted R^2 is .41, with an N of 100.

15. The question that was used to code position is: "What is your current position (for example, job captain, draftsman)?" Using standard references for office practice issued by the American Institute of Architects and consulting on occasion with officials in the Institute's local and national offices, a coding guide was prepared to code the detailed positions supplied by respondents. In cases of doubt, answers to another questionnaire item asking for chief responsibilities were examined.

16. The comparison involves three regression analyses based on managers ($N = 157$), staff designers ($N = 138$), and staff architects ($N = 83$). Other variables held constant in each analysis are: degree in architecture, the number of project types in which the architect has worked in the past year, membership in professional associations, professional activities outside the firm, years with the office, and firm size. A final technical point is warranted concerning the decision to use three regression analyses rather than an analysis of covariance (ANOC). The parsimony of ANOC is partly offset by the fact that it is less commonly used and therefore even sociologists encounter problems with interpretation. However, using the criterion provided by Schoenberg (1972) the results for the regressions are comparable to what would be obtained with ANOC. I accept as meaningful only a coefficient that when subtracted from another exceeds the sum of their standard errors. In the regression for managers, staff designers, and staff architects, the betas for work in diverse tasks, are, respectively, .26, .04, .06. Only that for managers is significant at at least the .05 level.

17. See note 16. The betas for work in peripheral specialities are: managers (.10), designers (.28), and staff architects (.26). Only the last two are significant. In these regressions there are additional findings that should be briefly noted. Only for managers does work on many different project types augment power (.26), which lends additional support to the conclusion that it is broad and general competence that provides managers with particularly much control. Qualifications (having an architecture degree) increase the likelihood of designers' exercising voice (beta = .23) but not of others. The lowest-ranking architects are unique in that the longer they work in the office, the more they exercise influence on decisions (beta = .27), which suggests that the power of lower participants depends in part on their established informal connections and knowledge about long-standing procedures.

18. These three areas were selected because architects consider them important; discussions about each of them tend to be intense and argumentative, which highlights their salience in the arena of office politics. None, however, reflects the extent to which the lowest-ranking professionals and nonprofessionals exercise voice. The correlations among the measures listed in the text, according to their numbers, are: 1 and 2, .20; 1 and 3, .16; 2 and 3, .08. Their low correlations indicate that these items tap different dimensions of participation.

19. "In charge" has two meanings: the legal right to sign the commission and final approval and the actual control of a project from beginning to end. It is the latter that was asked about in the interviews.

20. A total of 120 faculty members from five New York City schools of architecture rated firms on a five-point scale in terms of the quality of the firm's work. To spare each person the task of rating 152 offices, each of the firms was randomly assigned to one of four evaluation questionnaires. Thus each set of thirty-eight offices was evaluated by 30 faculty members.

21. Actual firm profits is confidential information. A good indicator, I was told by many practicing architects as well as officials of professional organizations, is construction costs, but they usually suggest costs at a higher cutoff point than $1 million. However, because in this analysis the interest is not those firms that are exceedingly profitable but rather how firms vary around a moderate level of profits, this particular indicator was chosen. An attempt to measure overhead by estimating rental costs in terms of office location in the city was not successful; office location has no relationship with construction costs.

22. The full definition and measurement of staff commitment is provided in chapter 3.

23. The correlations are in parentheses and the partial correlations are based on controls for log of size. The significance levels are .05(*) and .01(**). The results for decentralized client contact are: experts' evaluations (.25**), .14*; client repeat rate (.26**), .26**; construction costs (.37**), .29**.

24. See note 23. The results for "share responsibility for a project" are: client repeat rate (.30**), .30**; construction costs (.16*), .15*.

25. See note 23. The results for "decentralization of project control" are: experts' evaluations (.20**), .14*; client repeat rate (.35**), .30**; staff commitment (.24*), .22*.

26. See note 23. The results for "share responsibility for a project" are: awards (.08), −.18*. The results for decentralization of project control are: client referral rate (−.12), −.14*.

Chapter 3

1. An interesting account of the use of architecture and space in literature is found in Harbison (1977).

2. John Dewey (1958:203–231) comes close to the contemporary position in aesthetics: "That . . . ends enter organically into the structure of buildings seems too evident to permit of discussion. That degradation to some special use often occurs and is artistically detrimental is equally clear." It seems somewhat ironical that the major proponent of pragmatism should express a nonpractical view of buildings.

3. Questions were selected for the purpose of this study from a variety of sources: Aiken and Hage (1966), Seeman (1967), Miller (1967), Morse (1953). After appropriate modifications in wording, they were pretested in ten firms. Each question has four response categories (from 1, strongly disagree, to 4, strongly agree) without a category for a neutral response. Principal component factor analysis yielded four factors (the technique is comprehensively covered in Harman 1967). Each scale is based on the sum of the numerical scores of items that have loadings of at least .40 on the factor. The number of cases for the factor analysis and subsequent regressions reported in this chapter is 361 individuals.

4. Year of degree has moderate relationships with two scales, but both disappear under controls. Position is included in each analysis, to control its influence.

5. Size, comprehensive services, and client type are firm attributes that have significant simple correlations with one or more of the scales, yet none is significant under controls.

6. Career Contentment, although of primary substantive interest, is second in terms of its statistical importance, accounting for 13 percent of the variance.

7. Results of the regression for Career Contentment are reported as follows: Pearson correlation coefficient (in parentheses), beta coefficient, level of significance (.05 by one asterisk and .01 by two). These results are: number of tasks (.25), .19**; award-winning project (.12), .10*; power (.20), .12*; types of projects (.11), .10*; position as nonmanager (−.09), −.00. The R^2 is .31.

8. This factor accounts for 71 percent of the variance and is the most important of the four.

9. This scale is discussed in chapter 4.

10. See note 7. The results for Professional Egotism are: power (.20), .16*; user orientation (.14), .13*; number of tasks (.18), .13*; position as nonmanager (−.01), .00. The R^2 is .08.

11. This factor accounts for 9 percent of the variance.

12. See note 7. The results for Career Alienation are: user orientation (.12), .12*; number of tasks (.09), .11[n.s.]; nonmanager (−.09), −.09[n.s.]. The R^2 is .04.

13. This factor accounts for 7 percent of the variance. The item, "My work is my most rewarding experience," is included in scales of both Job Satisfaction and Career Contentment because of its high loadings on both factors (.45 and .54, respectively).

14. See note 7. The results for Job Satisfaction are: number of tasks (.29), .22**; power (.26), .15**; nonmanager (−.20), .07. The R^2 is .13.

15. In the interviews I attempted to ascertain the degree to which the office was organized along vertical or horizontal lines, but I failed. One difficulty is that most principals do not keep organization charts, so that their verbal descriptions of how work is organized yielded more information about architectural practice than about organization. The other difficulty is that the word *team* means both a kind of structure and comradeship. Every principal considers the firm to be characterized by good teamwork in the latter sense. Thus although I could not classify every office, many clear examples of the two types of organization could be identified, and in these I was able to obtain information from members concerning how the structure affected their work.

Chapter 4

1. I am aware of no single source for assembled materials on the architect in mythology, legend, and literature. The following sources, however, include interesting, if incomplete, discussions: Kris and Kurz (1979), Saint (1983), and Abell (1957).

2. This conceptualization derives in large part from McKeon's (1943–1944) analyses of Aristotle's four causes; also see Brumbaugh's (1947) summary.

3. That notion that ideas and beliefs are structured is advanced in several theories, including in Kuhn's (1974) work on the scientific paradigm. The relevance of a paradigm for art is discussed by Crane (1972), Ianni (1969), and Hafner (1969), as well as by Kuhn (1969). The significance of organized meanings is clear in structuralism (see Levi-Strauss 1967; Boudon 1971), in semiotics (de Saussure 1959; Barthes 1968; Eco 1980), and in the sociology of knowledge (Holzner and Marx 1979). Differences among these approaches are very important but not consequential for the problems addressed in this chapter. What is relevant and significant, however, is the extraordinary agreement among scholars holding different assumptions that unobservables—ideas and values—exhibit clear structure and pattern.

4. One speaker after another denounced the Fountainebleau Hotel, the location of an AIA convention, as "schmaltz"; when Morris Lapidus rose finally from the audience, he said, "Having fun, though, aren't you?" (Personal interview with Alan Lapidus.) The emphasis on color, strong light, curves, and ornament anticipated in certain ways the 1973 Hyatt Regency Hotel by Portman (see Davis 1973) and the more recent Yale building by Venturi (Goldberger 1983).

5. Using a matrix of Kendall tau coefficients as input, principal component analysis with orthogonal varimax rotation was the procedure used for the factor analysis.

6. The first factor accounts for 26 percent of the common variance; the next three each accounts for about 12 percent.

7. *American Institute of Architects Journal* (Spring 1980:69). Certainly critics, even some inside the profession, were vocal between 1974 to 1984 on issues pertaining to the environment, the aesthetic and functional context, and users' needs (see, for example, these issues of the *AIA Journal:* November 1976, October 1975, December 1974). Yet outside of design issues, the overriding concerns of the profession during this period, at least as reflected in journals, were marketing in a poor economy and energy-efficient buildings.

8. The procedure used was principal component analysis with varimax orthogonal rotation. A matrix of Spearman rho coefficients was used as input instead of a correlation matrix. Ten factors were extracted.

9. The first factor accounts for 18 percent of the common variance; the remaining seven reported account for about 10 percent each.

10. Because such a broad question could not be asked in a questionnaire, which heads of very small firms were sent in 1974, only firm heads of medium and large offices were asked about their agendas in the first study. In the ten pretest firms the question had not been asked, nor was it in those firms in which a partner not primarily concerned with project design was interviewed. This accounts for why the number of cases is 77 rather than 91 or 152. The principals of each surviving firm were asked the question in 1979 again unless the principal interviewed was not involved with project design.

11. These conclusions are based on an examination of the Pearson correlations between categories of agendas and aggregate measures of convictions for the members of the firm. Each aggregate measure was computed by summing each individual's score on the items in a given cluster and then obtaining a mean score for the firm. An aggregate score was computed only if the response rate for the office was at least 33 percent. An association is reported in these conclusions if the correlation between the two is significant beyond the level of .05.

Chapter 5

1. Columbia University's *Avery Index to Architectural Periodicals* was used for this purpose. It provides coverage of over a thousand journals.

2. This measure includes juried awards and competitions. To discourage estimates, each principal was asked to provide information on the source of the award, project name, and date.

3. The correlations are: between awards and journal articles, .73; between awards and average evaluation, .50; between journal articles and average evaluation, .72.

4. For example, a sociologist (John Zeisel) served on the 1974 Progressive Architecture award jury, a journalist (Barlay Gordon) appeared on the 1974 AIA residential award jury, and women were represented on most of the national and New York City juries. Of interest, too, are some of the recipients of awards: Gwathmey & Siegel, Mauer & Mauer (AIA residential awards); I. M. Pei, Holabird and Root, Mitchell/Giurgola, Richard Meier, Wolf Associates (AIA Honor awards). The local Fifth Avenue Association awarded Ivan

Chermayeff a street graphics award for his number "9" for 9 West Fifty-seventh Street, while the architects, SOM, were told by the jury that the building "has urban bad manners."

5. *Suppressor effect* is the term sociologists use for a relationship that is evident only when a third variable is controlled. For example, Rose (1952:128) found no connection between length of time in a union and tolerance toward Jews. Controlling age, however, he found a positive relationship. This is because younger members, who have not been in the union a long time, are the most tolerant. Seniority does increase tolerance, but age suppresses its effect. Because I report how a combination of variables rather than one variable is involved in concealing an effect and because it is not a strict causal model, the term *suppressor effect* would be misleading.

6. The technique used here is discriminant function analysis. It yields a function (or functions) consisting of a set of variables that together best discriminates between two (or more) groups—between, for example, firms in which profits are emphasized and those in which they are not. More precisely the function is a set of weighted variables that in linear combination maximally differentiates between the groups. In the analyses presented here each solution has only one function, and the interpretation of the results depends on the relative magnitudes of the product of each group's mean value on the function, or its centroid, and the standardized coefficients of the variables that make up the function. Values of centroids on the linear function range from +1.00 to −1.00, and values of the weighted values are standardized so they too range from +1.00 to −1.00. The method employed to enter variables is the conventional one; it is based on the minimization of Wilks' lambda, and the criterion for variable inclusion is a partial F ratio of 1.0. (See Cooley and Lohnes 1971:243–257; Klecka 1980; Morrison 1969; Tatsuoka 1971.) Exploratory work using multiple regression indicated that the same firm-level variables could be used for all three analyses involving agendas. Variables entered in each of the three are: Incorporation; Affiliate; Joint Ventures; Corporate Clients; Diverse Services; Size (log); Awards; Percentage Projects in New York City; Number of Rules; Staff Increase, 1973–1974; Survival. Although most are excluded in any given analyses, their initial inclusion makes the three comparisons meaningful.

7. The linkage diagrams in this chapter are schematic versions based on the results of the discriminant function analyses. The diagram for client satisfaction is based on the following statistical results: firms in which client satisfaction is a main orientation has a centroid (mean on the linear function) of .34 and ones without this orientation one of −.63; the function is defined by the following variables (standardized coefficients in parentheses): Incorporated (.50), Joint Ventures (.71), Percentage New York City Projects (.70), Log Size (.43), Awards (−.51). The function is significant at the .01 level. It is only if the firm's organization has these features—corporate status, many joint ventures, high proportion of local projects, large size—that an agenda relating to client satisfaction reduces award winning.

8. The discriminant function analysis on which the diagram is based provides the following results. Firms in which financial success is stressed has a centroid of .26 and ones in which it is not has a centroid of −.57 on the following function: Corporate Clients (.53), Percentage Projects in New York City (.49),

Staff Increase, 1973–1974 (−.45), Survival (.58), Awards (−.38). The function is significant at the .07 level.

9. The results of the discriminant function analysis on which the diagram is based are as follows. Firms in which aesthetics is stressed have a centroid of .71, and firms in which it is not have a centroid of −.28 on the following function: Affiliate (−.65), Percentage Engineers (−.35), Comprehensive Services (.33), Awards (.62). The function is significant at the .01 level.

10. The diagram is based on the following results of the discriminant function analysis. Those individuals ranking above the median on subjectivism have a centroid of .44, and those that rank below it have a centroid of −.47 on the following function of firm attributes: Corporate Clients (−.29), Age (−.43), Rules (−.29), Awards (.49). The function is significant beyond the .001 level. Percentage Engineers and Incorporation were included in the analysis but had no discriminatory power.

11. There is some evidence that the tendency for large firms to centralize decision making and to discourage wide participation also hurts the quality of their work (J. R. Blau 1976b). The measure of decision making is based on staff meetings, for which data are available for only fifty-eight firms. Otherwise the interaction effects are observed only for small firms.

12. Most of these differences, though substantial, are not significant at the .05 level. There is a small overall N, but the principle of eccentricity itself involves the rare firm and therefore tends to violate the assumption of equal Ns and variances, in a test of differences.

13. Number of awards won in the five years prior to 1979 was regressed on 1974 characteristics (for example, percentage private clients) and gain measures (for example, percentage private clients, 1979, minus percentage private clients, 1974, divided by percentage private clients, 1974). The trimmed equation yielded the following results as summarized by standardized coefficients and levels of significance in parentheses: 1974 size, .89 (.001), 1969–1973 productivity, −.50 (.001), percentage 1973 projects for which consultants are used, −.47 (.001), percentage staff in 1974 that are technicians, −.14 (.10), 1974 personnel rules, .23 (.01), gain in personnel rules, .12 (ns); diversity of clients, 1974, .11 (ns); gain in diversity of clients, .40 (.001), 1969–1973 awards, .05 (ns). The N is 78, and the adjusted R^2 is .61. Diversity of clients is computed as $1 - \Sigma p_i^2$; with i the nine categories of clients, and p the proportion of clients in a given category.

14. With statistical controls for size, firm age, profits, and use of consultants, the client repeat rate depends on the following factors (betas and significance levels reported): Percentage Private Clients, −.22 (.01); Number in Charge of Project, .18 (.05), Awards, −.32 (.02). The N is 132 and the adjusted R^2, .32.

15. Firms with high repeat rates are less likely to have commissions for residential projects (−.16) and more likely to design commercial projects (.29) but are not more or less likely to do industrial work (−.07).

16. Referral rate has a correlation of .11 with size and .16 with awards, neither of which is significant.

17. Referral rate depends on the following factors (betas and significance levels reported): Percentage Private Clients, .27 (.01); Informal Recruitment, .22 (.02); Joint Ventures, .23 (.02). The N is 130 and the adjusted R^2, .16.

18. Repeat rate and referral rate are correlated .16 and .10, respectively, with productivity. Firms with a high client repeat rate do tend to do large-scale projects, with construction costs of over $5 million ($r = .21$), but the connection is not causal, as both depend only on firm size.

19. This is Klingender's (1970) term to refer to the decline of English painting in the mid-eighteenth century that accompanied the rise of capitalists who possessed unlimited resources and exceedingly limited tastes.

Chapter 6

1. The correlation between age of firm and whether a firm had won an award for 1974 is .19; for 1979 the correlation is .07.

2. Figures for unemployment among the city's architects are not available, but after 1974, unemployment was estimated to be between one-quarter to one-third (AIA New York City chapter).

3. A reliable indication of an architecture firm's intactness proved to be the name of the office. Relatively minor changes sometimes occur with reorganization or on the death or departure of an owner or partner. Mergers tend to result in a significant change, and therefore two mergers that had come about because of pending insolvency of a sampled firm were defined as failures. Any Manhattan firm that relocated within another New York City borough was defined as a survivor.

4. The exceptional case is Caudill, Rowlett and Scott; it rejoined its larger Texas affiliate and for the purpose of this study becomes defined as a failing firm. It is the only example of successful relocation I discovered in interviews with architects.

5. Sixty-nine percent of award-winning firms survived; 55 percent of those that had not won awards did.

6. The correlation between percentage of projects that are medical centers or health facilities and survival is .24. Because theories concerning survival and failure proved to be of little use, I proceeded with the data analysis in a highly exploratory way. With the exception of awards, no other variable is significantly related to the dichotomous variable of failure-survival. This in itself is a statistical unlikelihood; on the basis of chance, ten out of one hundred relationships are expected to be significantly different from zero. Approximately 250 characteristics of firms were examined in this exploratory analysis. The relationships are negligible. To illustrate, the correlations of survival with Log of Size is .19; Percentage Private Clients, −.12; Corporate Status, .08; Joint Ventures, .05; Age of Firm, −.06; Comprehensive Services, .03; Number of Divisions, .08; Percentage Registered Architects, .13; Use of Consultants, .13. Moreover, further analyses yielded no appreciable interaction effects. I also examined the variances of characteristics of survivors and nonsurvivors to test the hypothesis that there was greater diversity among the survivors; there were essentially no significant differences.

7. See note 13 in chapter 5 for the measure of client diversity.

8. The matrix shown on the next page summarizes the relationships between strategies and changes in effectiveness, 1974–1979.

Effectiveness Relative Gain or Loss	Strategies					
	Reorganize	Leadership changes	Layoffs	Search for new clients	Introduce energy technology	Introduce renovation
Δ Size	.03	.14	-.19*	-.07	.01	.14
Δ Profits	.02	-.05	-.11	-.21*	.10	-.19*
Δ Productivity	.16	.04	.06	.18	-.07	-.05
Δ Awards	-.06	.07	.00	.16	-.02	-.06
Δ Client services	-.14	.14	-.13	-.00	.23*	-.19*
Δ Diverse clients	-.18	-.10	-.07	.12	-.09	-.15
Δ Percentage architects	-.01	-.19*	.15	.09	-.09	-.02
Δ Percentage nonlocal projects	.03	.17	-.11	.04	.01	-.05
Δ Repeat rate	-.04	-.07	.12	.16	-.13	.11

Note: Δ is the absolute difference between the level of a variable at 1979 and that at 1974, divided by the 1974 level.
*Significant at the .05 level.

9. Discriminant function analysis is used here to distinguish among the three groups in each of these comparisons. See note 6 to chapter 5.

10. Figure 6.1 summarizes the results for an analysis of profits using discriminant function analysis (DFA). The group centroids fall in a curvilinear pattern on the single function that best discriminates among them. The values of the centroids are: Failures (−.41), Profits Stable or Decline (.53), Profits Increase (.18). The values of the standardized coefficients are: Affiliate (.68); Log of Size (.50); Percentage Local Projects (.47); Referral Rate (−.41); Corporate Clients (.18); Percentage Projects Use Consultants (.11). The function is significant beyond the .01 level.

11. Productivity and profits are correlated −.01 in 1974, and among surviving firms in 1979 they are correlated .11.

12. Figure 6.2 summarizes the results for an analysis of productivity using DFA. The curvilinear pattern is revealed in the values of the centroids: Failures (−.34), Productivity Stable or Decline (.59), and Productivity Increases (−.12). The function is defined by the standardized coefficients of the following variables: Percentage Corporate Clients (.69), Log of Size (.48), Number of Client Services (−.42), Computer (.33), and Diverse Projects (.27). (Diverse Projects is measured by the proportion of fifty-three distinct project types that firms had as commissioned work and completed during 1973.) The function is significant beyond the .01 level.

13. Figure 6.3 summarizes the results for an analysis of growth using DFA. The centroids are curvilinear with respect to the function: Failures (.14), Stable or Decline in Size (−.53), and Growth (.32). The function is described by the standardized coefficients of the following variables: Percentage Architects (.87), Diverse Projects (−.62), Percentage Corporate Clients (.46). Thus the two extreme categories have relatively large professional components, specialize in a few project types, and have disproportionately many corporate clients. The function is significant beyond the .01 level.

14. Having a large architectural component is negatively related to Percentage Corporate Clients (−.16), Corporate Status (−.26), Affiliate Status (−.27), Number of Distinct Departments (−.36), and an indicator of Internal Bureaucratization, Number of Operating Rules (−.39). These correlations, for the 1974 data, are all significant beyond the .05 level.

15. Firms with high profits in 1974 tended, for example, to be very large ($r = .59$), unlikely to be a sole proprietorship ($r = −.42$), with few private clients (−.36), and they presumably benefited financially by employing large numbers of technicians (.24) and by using outside consultants (.28). Firms with high productivity records in 1974 tended to be large (.33), relied on corporate clients (.31), and although they were not more likely to be corporate firms (.06), they were more often corporate affiliates (.19). In contrast to profits, productivity is related to formalization—that is, rules and regulations (.31) and computer technology (.17). Not all of these factors persists to influence either productivity or profits, but no curvilinear effects were revealed in interaction analysis, in contrast to the analyses of changes presented in this chapter. In criticism of my earlier work (Blau and Lieben 1983) I must note that initially productivity change was not found to yield a curvilinear pattern.

Subsequent data analysis of interaction effects, guided by the assumptions outlined in this chapter, indicated an incorrectly specified model. Otherwise these subsequent analyses confirm the findings we report there.

Chapter 7

1. Paul Rudolph, quoted in Cranston Jones (1961:175). Such a statement is not atypical; see discussions by Gehry (Diamonstein 1980:40), Paolo Soleri (Heyer 1966:81), and Victor Lundy (Cranston Jones 1961:175). As Saint (1983:14) notes, the role of the individualistic designer is gradually whittled away with the increasing complexity of practice, but the concept thrives, attached to the charismatic basis of high art.

References

Abell, Walter. 1957. *The Collective Dream in Art.* New York: Schocken.

Abrahamsson, Bengt. 1977. *Bureaucracy or Participation.* Beverly Hills: Sage.

Adler, Judith E. 1979. *Artists in Offices.* New Brunswick, N.J.: Transaction.

Aiken, Michael, and Jerald Hage. 1966. "Organizational alienation." *Administrative Science Quarterly* 31:497–507.

Aiken, Michael, and Jerald Hage. 1968. "Organizational interdependence and intra-organizational structure." *American Sociological Review* 33:912–929.

Aldrich, Howard E. 1979. *Organizations and Environments.* Englewood Cliffs, N.J.: Prentice-Hall.

Althusser, Louis. 1971. *Lenin and Philosophy and Other Essays.* London: New Left Books.

American Institute of Architects. 1973. "Graduate-practitioner: how far apart?" *Journal of the American Institute of Architects* 60:11–31.

American Institute of Architects. 1975. "Survey of firms chart decline in employment." *Journal of the American Institute of Architects* 64:41–42.

American Institute of Architects. 1977. "Survey finds architectural employment at stand still." *Journal of the American Institute of Architects* 66:20, 24.

American Institute of Architects, n.d. *Handbook.* Washington, D.C.: AIA.

Andrews, Wayne. 1964 [1947]. *Architecture, Ambition and Americans.* New York: Free Press.

Andrzejewski, Stanislaw. 1949. "Are ideas social forces?" *American Sociological Review* 14:758–764.

Antal, Frederick. 1966. *Classicism and Romanticism.* New York: Basic Books.

Arian, Edward. 1971. *Bach, Beethoven and Bureaucracy.* University: University of Alabama Press.

Arrow, Kenneth J. 1974. *The Limits of Organization.* New York: W. W. Norton.

Averitt, Robert. 1968. *The Dual Economy.* New York: W. W. Norton.

Babbage, Charles. 1963. [1832]. *On the Economy of Machinery and Manufactures.* London: C. Knight.

Bachner, John Philip, and Naresh Kumar Khusla. 1977. *Marketing and Promotion for Design Professionals.* New York: Van Nostrand.

Bailey, James. 1975. "Profile—AIA's new president, William Marshal." *American Institute of Architects Journal* 64:23.

Banham, Reyner. 1980. [1960]. *Theory and Design in the First Machine Age.* 2d ed. Cambridge: MIT Press.

Banham, Reyner, and C. Price. 1960. "Fold, Like the Arab." *Architects Journal* 131 (September):415.

Barnett, Jonathan. 1974. *Urban Design as Public Housing.* New York: Architectural Record.

Barthes, Roland. 1968. *Elements of Semiology.* Translated by Annette Lavers and Colin Smith. New York: Hill & Wang.

Beck, E. M., Patrick M. Horan, and Charles M. Tolbert II. 1980. "Industrial segmentation and labor market discrimination." *Social Problems* 28:113–130.

Becker, Howard S. 1974. "Art as collective action." *American Sociological Review* 39:767–776.

Becker, Howard S. 1982. *Art Worlds.* Berkeley: University of California Press.

Becker, Howard S., Blanche Geer, Everett C. Hughes, and Anselm Strauss. 1961. *Boys in White.* Chicago: University of Chicago Press.

Benson, J. Kenneth, and Jems H. Dorset. 1971. "Toward a theory of religious organizations." *Journal for the Study of Religion* 10:138–151.

Berger, Joseph, Susan J. Rosenholtz, and Morris Zelditch. 1980. "Status organizing processes." In Alex Inkeles, Neil J. Smelser, and Ralph H. Turner, eds., *Annual Review of Sociology,* Vol. 6. Palo Alto: Annual Reviews.

Berkeley, Ellen Perry. 1968. "Neighborhood Muse." *Architectural Forum* 129 (September):87.

Beyer, Janice M. 1982. "Ideologies, values, and decision making in organizations." In Paul C. Nystrom and William H. Starbuck, eds., *Handbook of Organizational Design.* Vol. 2. Oxford: Oxford University Press.

Bill, Max. 1954. "Report on Brazil." *Architectural Review* 116 (October):238, 239.

Blake, Peter. 1973. "I. M. Pei & Partners." *Architecture Plus* 1 (February):52–59 (March):21–25.

Blau, Judith R. 1976a. "Scientific recognition." *Social Studies of Science* 6:533–545.

Blau, Judith R. 1976b. "Beautiful buildings and breaching the laws." *Revue Internationale de Sociologie* 12:110–128.

Blau, Judith R. 1980. "Paradoxical consequences of excess in structural complexity." *Sociology of Health and Illness* 2:277–292.

Blau, Judith R., and Richard Alba. 1982. "Empowering nets of participation." *Administrative Science Quarterly* 27:363–379.

Blau, Judith R., and Katharyn Lieben. 1983. "Growth, decline, and death." In Judith R. Blau, Mark La Gory, and John S. Pipkin, eds., *Professionals and Urban Form.* Albany: State University of New York Press.

Blau, Judith R., Mark La Gory, and John S. Pipkin, eds. 1983. *Professionals and Urban Form.* Albany: State University of New York Press.

Blau, Peter M. 1968. "The hierarchy of authority in organizations." *American Journal of Sociology* 73:453–467.

Blau, Peter M. 1973. *The Organization of Academic Work*. New York: Wiley.

Blau, Peter M., and Richard Schoenherr. 1971. *The Structure of Organizations*. New York: Basic Books.

Bonta, Juan. 1980. "Notes for a theory of meaning in design." In Geoffrey Broadbent, Richard Bunt, and Charles Jencks, eds., *Signs, Symbols, and Architecture*. New York: Wiley.

Boudon, Raymond. 1971. *The Uses of Structuralism*. London: Heinemann.

Boyle, Bernard Michael. 1977. "Architectural practice in America, 1865–1965." In Spiro Kostof, ed., *The Architect*. New York: Oxford University Press.

Braverman, Harry. 1974. *Labor and Monopoly Capital*. New York: Monthly Review Press.

Brett, Lionel. 1971. *Architecture in a Crowded World*. New York: Schocken.

Brewer, John. 1972. "Organizations/occupations interface: the case of autonomy and organizational authority in architecture." Paper presented at the American Sociological Association Meetings.

Broadbent, Geoffrey. 1980. "The deep structures of architecture." In Geoffrey Broadbent, Richard Bunt, and Charles Jencks, eds., *Signs, Symbols, and Architecture*. New York: Wiley.

Broady, Maurice. 1973. "Sociology in the education of architects." *Architecture Association Quarterly* 5:49–52.

Brolin, Brent C. 1976. *The Failure of Modern Architecture*. New York: Van Nostrand Reinhold.

Brumbaugh, Robert S. 1947. "Broad and narrow-context techniques of literary criticism." *English Journal* 36:293–299.

Burchard, John, and Albert Bush-Brown. 1966. [1961]. *The Architecture of America*. Abridged ed. Boston: Little, Brown.

Carmon, Naomi, and Mannheim, Bilha. 1979. "Reference groups and professional self image." *Journal of Vocational Behavior* 14:169–180.

Cary, Joyce. 1958. *Art and Reality*. New York: Harper.

Caudill, William Wayne. 1971. *Architecture by Team*. New York: Van Nostrand.

Chandler, Alfred. 1962. *Strategy and Structure*. Cambridge: MIT Press.

Chermayeff, Serge, and Christopher Alexander. 1963. *Community and Privacy*. Garden City: Doubleday.

Child, John. 1972. "Organization structure, environment, and performance—the role of strategic choice." *Sociology* 6:1–22.

Clegg, Stewart, and David Dunkerley. 1980. *Organization, Class and Control*. London: Routledge & Kegan Paul.

Colbert, Charles. 1966. "Naked utility and visual chorea." In Laurence B. Holland, ed., *Who Designs America?* Garden City, N.Y.: Anchor.

Condit, Carl W. 1964. *The Chicago School of Architecture*. Chicago: University of Chicago Press.

Cook, John W., and Heinrick Klotz. 1973. *Conversations with Architects.* New York: Praeger.

Cooley, William W., and Paul R. Lohnes. 1971. *Multivariate Data Analysis.* New York: Wiley.

Crane, Diana. 1972. *Invisible College.* Chicago: University of Chicago Press.

Crozier, Michael. 1964. *The Bureaucratic Phenomenon.* Chicago: University of Chicago Press.

Cullen, John. 1983. "Structural aspects of the architectural profession." In Judith R. Blau, Mark La Gory, and John Pipkin, eds., *Professions of Urban Form.* Albany: State University of New York Press.

Curtis, William J. 1983. *Modern Architecture since 1900.* Englewood Cliffs, N.J.: Prentice-Hall.

Danto, Arthur C. 1964. "The artworld." *Journal of Philosophy* 61:571–584.

Danto, Arthur C. 1981. *The Transfiguration of the Common Place.* Cambridge: Harvard University Press.

Davis, Douglas. 1973. "Spaces for time." *Newsweek,* December 24, pp. 76–79.

Davis, Douglas. 1976. "Battle of the buildings." *Newsweek,* June 21, pp. 85, 87.

Deasy, C. M. 1974. *Design for Human Affairs.* Cambridge, Mass.: Schenckman.

Deeks, John. 1976. *The Firm Owner-Manager.* New York: Praeger.

Deinhard, Hanna. 1970. *Meaning and Expression.* Boston: Beacon Press.

Dewey, John. 1958. [1934]. *Art as Experience.* New York: Capricorn.

Diamonstein, Barbarlee. 1980. *American Architecture Now.* New York: Rizzoli.

Drexler, Arthur, and Thomas S. Hines. 1982. *The Architecture of Richard Neutra.* New York: Museum of Modern Art.

Drucker, Peter F. 1954. *The Practice of Management.* New York: Harper.

Eckstein, Harry. 1966. *Division and Cohesion in Democracy.* Princeton: Princeton University Press.

Eco, Umberto. 1980. [1972]. "A componential analysis of the architectural sign/column." In Geoffrey Broadbent, Richard Bunt, and Charles Jencks, eds., *Signs, Symbols, and Architecture.* New York: Wiley.

Edwards, Richard. 1979. *Contested Terrain.* New York: Basic Books.

Emerson, Richard M. 1962. "Power-dependence relations." *American Sociological Review* 27:31–40.

Etzkorn, K. Peter. 1973. "On the sphere of social validity in African art." In Warren L. d'Azevedo, ed., *The Traditional Artist in African Societies.* Bloomington: Indiana University Press.

Evan, William M. 1971. "The organization-set: toward a theory of interorganizational relations." In J. G. Maurer, ed., *Readings in Organization Theory.* New York: Random House.

Faulkner, Robert. 1973. "Orchestra interaction." *Sociological Quarterly* 14:147–157.

Faulkner, Robert R. 1983. *Music on Demand.* New Brunswick, N.J.: Transaction Books.

Fischer, Ernst. 1963. [1959]. *The Necessity of Art.* Harmondsworth: Penguin.

Fitch, James Marston. 1966. [1947]. *American Building.* Vol. 1: *The Historical Forces That Shaped It.* 2d ed. New York: Schocken.

Foster, Arnold W. 1976. "The slow radical." *British Journal of Aesthetics* 16:161–169.

Frampton, Kenneth. 1980. *Modern Architecture.* New York: Oxford University Press, 1980.

Freidson, Eliot. 1971. "Professions and the occupational principle." In Eliot Freidson, ed., *The Professions and their Prospects.* Beverley Hills: Sage.

Friedman, Yona. 1975. *Toward a Scientific Architecture.* Translated by Cynthia Lang. Cambridge: MIT Press.

Friedman, Yona. 1983. "Architecture by yourself." In Judith R. Blau, Mark La Gory, and John S. Pipkin, eds., *Professionals and Urban Form.* Albany: State University of New York Press.

Fuller, Peter. 1983. *The Naked Artist.* London: Writers & Readers Publishing Cooperative Society.

Gans, Herbert J. 1967. *The Levittowners.* New York: Pantheon.

Gans, Herbert J. 1968. *People and Plans.* New York: Basic Books.

Gans, Herbert J. 1982. [1962]. *The Urban Villagers.* New York: Free Press.

Garroni, Emilio. 1980. "The 'language' of architecture." In Geoffrey Broadbent, Richard Bunt, and Charles Jencks, eds., *Signs, Symbols, and Architecture.* New York: Wiley.

Giedion, Sigfried. 1971. *Architecture and the Phenomena of Transition.* Cambridge: Harvard University Press.

Gimpel, Jean. 1961. *The Cathedral Builders.* New York: Grove.

Goldberger, Paul. 1974. "Women architects building influence in a profession that is 98.8% male." *New York Times,* May 18, p. 33.

Goldberger, Paul. 1975. "For the architect, New York is home." *New York Times,* April 16, p. 43.

Goldberger, Paul. 1976a. "Two views of Chicago-school architects." *New York Times,* June 1, p. 50.

Goldberger, Paul. 1976b. "Debate lingers after the Beaux Arts show." *New York Times,* January 6, p. 38.

Goldberger, Paul. 1983. "Small building, big gestures." *New York Times,* June 19, pp. 35, 36.

Gombrich, E. H. 1951. "Meditations on a hobby horse or the roots of artistic form." In Lancelot Law Whyte, ed., *Aspects of Form.* London: Lund Humphries.

Goode, William J. 1957. "Community within a community." *American Sociological Review* 22:194–199.

Goodman, Robert. 1971. *After the Planners.* New York: Simon & Schuster.

Gordon, David M. 1972. *Theories of Poverty and Underemployment.* Lexington, Mass.: D. C. Heath.

Gordon, Whitney. n.d. "Ten years of looking at architects and nary a woman in the lot." Unpublished paper.

Gowans, Alan. 1970. *The Unchanging Arts.* Philadelphia: J. B. Lippincott.

Gropius, Walter. 1962. [1943]. *Scope of Total Architecture.* New York: Collier.

Gulick, Luther, and L. Urwick, eds. 1937. *Papers on the Science of Administration.* New York: Institute of Public Administration.

Gutman, Robert. 1972. *People and Buildings.* New York: Basic Books.

Gutman, Robert. 1977. "Architecture: the entrepreneurial profession." *Progressive Architecture* 58:55–58.

Gutman, Robert. 1983. "Architects in the home-building industry." In Judith R. Blau, Mark La Gory, and John Pipkin, eds., *Professionals of Urban Form.* Albany: State University of New York Press.

Hafner, E. M. 1969. "The new reality in art and science." *Comparative Studies in Society and History* 11:385–397.

Hage, Jerald. 1980. *Theories of Organizations.* New York: Wiley.

Hage, Jerald, and Michael Aiken. 1970. *Social Change in Complex Organizations.* New York: Random House.

Hall, Richard H. 1968. "Professionalization and bureaucracy." *American Sociological Review* 33:92–104.

Hannan, Michael, and John Freeman. 1977. "The population ecology of organizations." *American Journal of Sociology* 82:929–64.

Harbison, Robert. 1977. *Eccentric Spaces.* New York: Alfred A. Knopf.

Harman, Harry H. 1967. *Modern Factor Analysis.* Chicago: University of Chicago Press.

Hauser, Arnold. 1951. *The Social History of Art.* 4 vols. New York: Vintage.

Hayden, Dolores. 1981. *The Grand Domestic Revolution.* Cambridge: MIT Press.

Hershberger, Robert. 1969. *A Study of Meaning in Architecture.* Philadelphia: Institute of Environmental Studies, University of Pennsylvania.

Heydebrand, Wolf V. 1981. "Marxist structuralism." In Peter M. Blau and Robert K. Merton, eds., *Continuities in Structural Inquiry.* Beverly Hills: Sage.

Heydebrand, Wolf V. 1983a. "Technocratic Corporatism." In Richard Hall and Robert Quinn, eds., *Organizational Theory and Public Policy.* Beverly Hills: Sage.

Heydebrand, Wolf V. 1983b. "The technocratic administration of higher education." Unpublished paper.

Heyer, Paul. 1966. *Architects on Architecture.* New York: Walker and Co.

Hickson, David J., C. R. Hinings, C. A. Lee, R. E. Schneck, and J. M. Pennings. 1971. "A strategic contingencies' theory of interorganizational power." *Administrative Science Quarterly* 16:216–229.

Hill, Stephen. 1981. *Competition and Control at Work.* Cambridge: MIT Press.

Hinings, C. R., D. J. Hickson, J. M. Pennings, and R. E. Schneck. 1974. "Structural conditions of intraorganization power." *Administrative Science Quarterly* 19:22–44.

Hirsch, Paul M. 1975. "Organizational effectiveness and the institutional environment." *Administrative Science Quarterly* 20:327–344.

Hitchcock, Henry-Russell. 1968. *Architecture, Nineteenth and Twentieth Centuries.* Harmondsworth: Penguin.

Hodgkinson, Christopher. 1978. *Toward a Philosophy of Administration*. Oxford: Basil Blackwood.

Holzner, Burkart, and John H. Marx. 1979. *Knowledge Application*. Boston: Allyn and Bacon.

Hubbard, William. 1980. *Complicity and Conviction*. Cambridge: MIT Press.

Hughes, Everett Cherrington. 1958. *Men and Their Work*. Glencoe, Ill.: Free Press.

Hughes, Robert. 1981. *The Shock of the New*. New York: Alfred A. Knopf.

Huizinga, Johan. 1955. *Homo Ludens*. Boston: Beacon Press.

Huxtable, Ada Louise. 1974. "The letterhead is solidly male." *New York Times,* May 19, p. 8.

Huxtable, Ada Louise. 1975. "Crisis in modern architecture." *New York Review of Books,* November 27, pp. 6, 8, 10.

Huxtable, Ada Louise. 1976. "The gospel according to Giedion and Gropius is under attack." *New York Times,* June 27.

Huxtable, Ada Louise. 1983. "After modern architecture." *New York Review of Books,* December 8, pp. 29–35.

Ianni, Lawrence A. 1969. "Science and art as forms of communication." *Arts in Society* 6:165–175.

Jacobs, Jane. 1961. *The Death and Life of Great American Cities*. New York: Vintage Books.

Jencks, Charles A. 1971. *Architecture 2000*. New York: Praeger.

Jencks, Charles A. 1973. *Modern Movements in Architecture*. New York: Doubleday.

Jencks, Charles A. 1981. *The Language of Post-Modern Architecture*. Rev. ed. New York: Rizzoli.

Jenkins, Frank. 1961. *Architect and Patron*. London: Oxford University Press.

Joedicke, Jürgen. 1969. *Architecture since 1945*. London: Paul Mall.

Johnson, Philip. 1973. "We still have an art of architecture—and now where do we go with it?" *Inland Architect* (February):14–19.

Jones, Christopher. 1970. *Design Methods*. New York: Wiley.

Jones, Cranston. 1961. *Architecture Today and Tomorrow*. New York: McGraw-Hill.

Jones, Gerre L. 1973. *How to Market Professional Design Services*. New York: McGraw-Hill.

Jordy, William H. 1976. *American Buildings and Their Architects*. Vol. 3. Garden City, N.Y.: Doubleday.

Kahn, Louis I. 1975. [1960]. "Order is." In Ulrich Conrads, ed., *Programs and Manifestoes on 20th-Century Architecture*. Cambridge: MIT Press.

Kant, Immanuel. 1952. [1790]. *The Critique of Judgement*. Oxford: Oxford University Press.

Kanter, Rosabeth Moss. 1977. *Men and Women of the Corporation*. New York: Basic Books.

Kaplan, Abraham. 1964. "Power in perspective." In Robert L. Kahn and Elise Boulding, eds., *Power and Conflict in Organizations.* New York: Basic Books.

Karpik, Lucien. 1978. *Organizations and Environment.* Beverly Hills: Sage.

Katz, Daniel, and Robert L. Kahn. 1966. *The Social Psychology of Organizations.* New York: Wiley.

Kaufman, Herbert. 1976. *Are Government Organizations Immortal?* Washington, D.C.: Brookings Institute.

Kaye, Barrington. 1960. *The Development of the Architectural Profession in Britain.* London: Allen and Unwin.

Keller, Suzanne. 1968. *The Urban Neighborhood.* New York: Random House.

Kirby, Michael. 1967. "The experience of kinesis." In Thomas B. Hess and John Ashbery, eds. *The Avant Garde.* London: Collier-Macmillan.

Klecka, William R. 1980. *Discriminant Analysis.* Beverly Hills: Sage.

Klingender, F. D. 1970. [1947]. *Art and the Industrial Revolution.* Ed. and rev. ed. Arthur Elton. New York: Schocken.

Knight, Frank. 1956. *On the History and Method of Economics.* Chicago: Phoenix.

Knight, Frank. 1965. *Risk, Uncertainty, and Profit.* New York: Harper & Row.

Kornhauser, William. 1963. *Scientists in Industry.* Berkeley: University of California Press.

Kostof, Spiro, ed. 1977. *The Architect.* New York: Oxford University Press.

Kraft, Philip. 1977. *Programmers and Managers.* New York: Springer-Verlag.

Kris, Ernst, and Otto Kurz. 1979. *Legend, Myth and Magic in the Image of the Artist.* New Haven: Yale University Press.

Kron, Joan. 1980. "The almost-perfect life of Denise Scott Brown." *Savvy* (December):28–35.

Kuhn, Thomas S. 1969. "Comment." *Comparative Studies in Science and History* 11:403–412.

Kuhn, Thomas S. 1974. [1970]. *The Structure of Scientific Revolution.* Chicago: University of Chicago Press.

La Gory, Mark, and John Pipkin. 1981. *Urban Social Space.* Belmont, Calif.: Wadsworth.

Langer, Suzanne K. 1957. *Problems of Art.* New York: Charles Scribner's Sons.

Langer, Suzanne. 1966. "The social influence of design." In Laurence B. Holland, ed., *Who Designs America?* Garden City, N.Y.: Anchor.

Larson, Magali Sarfatti. 1977. *The Rise of Professionalism.* Berkeley: University of California Press.

Larson, Magali Sarfatti. 1980. "Proletarianization and educated labor." *Theory and Society* 9:131–176.

Larson, Magali Sarfatti. 1983. "Emblem and exception: the historical definition of the architect's professional role." In Judith R. Blau, Mark La Gory, and John S. Pipkin, eds., *Professionals and Urban Form.* Albany: State University of New York Press.

Larson, Magali Sarfatti, George Leon, and Jay Bollick. 1983. "The professional supply of design." In Judith R. Blau, Mark La Gory, and John S. Pipkin, eds., *Professionals and Urban Form*. Albany: State University of New York Press.

Lazarsfeld, Paul F. 1955. "Interpretation of statistical relationships." In Paul F. Lazarsfeld and Morris Rosenberg, eds., *The Language of Social Research*. Glencoe, Ill.: Free Press.

Lévi-Strauss, Claude. 1967. *Structural Anthropology*. Garden City, N.Y.: Doubleday Anchor.

Liebert, Roland J. 1976. *Disintegration and Political Action*. New York: Academic Press.

Lindenfeld, F., and Joyce Rothschild-Whitt, eds. 1979. *Workplace Democracy and Social Change*. Boston: Porter Sargent.

Lipman, Alan. 1969. "The architectural belief system and social behavior." *British Journal of Sociology* 20:190–204.

Lynch, Kevin. 1960. *The Image of the City*. Cambridge: MIT Press.

MacDonald, William L. 1977. "Roman architects." In Spiro Kostof, ed., *The Architect*. New York: Oxford University Press.

McKeon, Richard. 1943–1944. "Philosophic bases of art and criticism." *Modern Philology* 41:65–87, 129–171.

MacKinnon, Donald W. 1962. "The personality correlates of creativity." *Proceedings of the Fourteenth Congress on Applied Psychology*. Vol. 2. Munksgaard.

MacKinnon, Donald W. 1965. "Personality and the realization of creative potential." *American Psychologist* 20:273–281.

Mandel, Ernest. 1975. *Late Capitalism*. London: New Left Books.

Manfredi, John. 1982. *The Social Limits of Art*. Amherst: University of Massachusetts Press.

Mann, Dennis Alan. 1978. "Why be original when you can be good." *Journal of American Culture* 1:217–236.

Marcuse, Herbert. 1978. *The Aesthetic Dimension*. Boston: Beacon Press.

Martorella, Rosanne. 1982. *The Sociology of Opera*. South Hadley, Mass.: J. F. Bergin.

Massie, Joseph F. 1965. "Management theory." In James G. March, ed., *Handbook of Organizations*. Chicago: Rand McNally.

Meadows, Paul. 1983. "Cities and professionals." In Judith R. Blau, Mark La Gory, and John Pipkin, eds., *Professionals and Urban Form*. Albany: State University of New York Press.

Melman, Seymour. 1951. "The rise in administrative overhead in the manufacturing industries of the United States, 1899–1947." *Oxford Economic Series* 3:62–112.

Michelson, William. 1976. *Man and His Environment*. Reading, Mass.: Addison-Wesley.

Miles, Robert H. 1982. *Coffin Nails and Corporate Strategies*. Englewood Cliffs, N.J.: Prentice-Hall.

Miller, George A. 1967. "Professionals in bureaucracy." *American Sociological Review* 32:755–768.

Mitchell, Howard. 1974. "Professional and client." In Jon Lang, Charles Burnette, Walter Moleski, and David Vachon, eds., *Designing for Human Behavior.* Stroudsburg, Pa.: Dowden, Hutchinson & Ross.

Moch, Michael K., and Edward V. Morse. 1977. "Size, centralization and organizational adoption of innovations." *American Sociological Review* 42:716–725.

Moholy-Nagy, Laszlo. 1946. [1928]. "Abstract of an artist." *The New Vision.* New York: Wittenborn.

Moore, Charles W. 1968. "How it looks to a critic." *Architectural Forum* 128 (June):76–79.

Moore, Gary T. 1970. *Emerging Methods in Environmental Design and Planning.* Cambridge: MIT Press.

Morawski, Stefan. 1974. *Inquiries into the Fundamentals of Aesthetics.* Cambridge: MIT Press.

Morrison, Donald G. 1969. "On the interpretation of discriminant analysis." *Journal of Marketing Research* 6:156–163.

Morse, Nancy C. 1953. *Satisfaction in the White Collar Job.* Ann Arbor: University of Michigan Press.

Mumford, Lewis. 1931. *The Brown Decades.* New York: Dover.

Mumford, Lewis. 1938. *The Culture of Cities.* New York: Harcourt, Brace.

Mumford, Lewis. 1947. *From the Ground Up.* New York: Harcourt, Brace.

Mumford, Lewis. 1954. "The life, teaching and the architecture of Matthew Nowicki." *Architectural Record* 116 (August):169–175.

Mumford, Lewis. 1959. "A backward glance." In Lewis Mumford, ed., *Roots of Contemporary Architecture.* New York: Grove Press.

Muschamp, Herbert. 1974. *File under Architecture.* Cambridge: MIT Press.

Nash, Dennison. 1955. "Challenge and response in the American composer's career." *Journal of Aesthetics and Art Criticism* 14:116–122.

Norberg-Schulz, Christian. 1963. *Intentions in Architecture.* Oslo: Universitetsforlaget. MIT Press edition, 1968.

Osborn, Richard N., and James G. Hunt. 1974. "Environment and organizational effectiveness." *Administrative Science Quarterly* 19:231–246.

Osman, Mary E. 1974. "The Case survey." *American Institute of Architects Journal* 65 (September):38–39, 65.

Palumbo, Dennis J. 1969. "Power and role specificity in organization theory." *Public Administration Review* 29:237–248.

Pateman, Carole. 1970. *Participation and Democratic Theory.* Cambridge: Cambridge University Press.

Paulson, Steven K. 1974. "Causal analysis of interorganizational relations." *Administrative Science Quarterly* 19:319–337.

Pelles, Geraldine. 1963. *Art, Artists and Society.* Englewood Cliffs, N.J.: Prentice-Hall.

Perin, Constance. 1970. *With Man in Mind.* Cambridge: MIT Press.

Perrow, Charles. 1972. *Complex Organizations.* Glenview, Ill.: Scott Foresman.

Perrucci, Robert. 1971. "Engineering: professional servant of power." In Elliot Freidson, ed., *Professions and Their Prospects*. Beverly Hills: Sage.

Perrucci, Robert, and Joel E. Gerstl. 1969. *Profession without Community*. New York: Random House.

Peterson, Richard A., and David G. Berger. 1971. "Entrepreneurship in organizations." *Administrative Science Quarterly* 16:97–107.

Pevsner, Nicholas. 1960. [1936]. *Pioneers of Modern Design*. Harmondsworth: Penguin.

Pfeffer, Jeffrey. 1972. "Merger as a response to organizational interdependence." *Administrative Science Quarterly* 17:382–394.

Pipkin, John S., Mark La Gory, and Judith R. Blau, eds. 1983. *Remaking the City*. Albany: State University of New York Press.

Ponti, Gio. *In Praise of Architecture*. New York: McGraw-Hill.

Read, Herbert. 1966. [1936]. *Art and Society*. New York: Schocken.

Richards, J. M. 1970. [1940]. *An Introduction to Modern Architecture*. Harmondsworth: Penguin.

Rock, David. 1973. "Setting up a practice." *Architect* 3 (March):80–82.

Rogers, Maria. 1970. [1959]. "The Batignolles group." In Milton C. Albrecht, James H. Barnett, and Mason Griff, eds., *The Sociology of Art and Literature*. New York: Praeger.

Rose, Arnold M. 1952. *Union Solidarity*. Minneapolis: University of Minnesota Press.

Rosenberg, Bernard, and Norris Fliegel. 1965. *The Vanguard Artist*. Chicago: Quadrangle.

Rosenberg, Deena, and Bernard Rosenberg. 1979. *The Music Makers*. New York: Columbia University Press.

Rosenberg, Harold. 1964. *The Anxious Object*. New York: Horizon Press.

Rosenberg, Morris. 1957. *Occupations and Values*. Glencoe, Ill.: Free Press.

Rosenthal, Robert. 1968. *Pygmalion in the Classroom*. New York: Holt, Rinehart & Winston.

Ross, Stephen David. 1982. *A Theory of Art*. Albany: State University of New York Press.

Rothschild-Whitt, Joyce. 1979. "The collectivist organization." *American Sociological Review* 44:509–528.

Rudofsky, Bernard. 1964. *Architecture without Architects*. Garden City, N.Y.: Doubleday.

Saint, Andrew. 1983. *The Image of the Architect*. New Haven: Yale University Press.

Salaman, Graeme. 1974. *Community and Occupation*. Cambridge: Cambridge University Press.

Salancik, Gerald R., Jeffrey Pfeffer, and J. Patrick Kelly. 1978. "A contingency model of influence on organizational decision-making." *Pacific Sociological Review* 21:239–256.

Salvadori, Mario. 1980. *Why Buildings Stand Up*. New York: W. W. Norton.

Santayana, George. 1955. *The Sense of Beauty*. New York: Modern Library.

Sarton, George. 1957. *Six Wings: Men of Science in the Renaissance.* Bloomington: Indiana University Press.

Saussure, de, Ferdinand. 1959. *Course in General Linguistics.* New York: Philosophical Library.

Schapiro, Meyer. 1953. "Style." In A. L. Kroeber, ed., *Anthropology Today.* Chicago: University of Chicago Press.

Schapiro, Meyer. 1978. *Modern Art.* New York: George Braziller.

Schattschneider, E. E. 1960. *The Semi-Sovereign People.* New York: Holt, Rinehart & Winston.

Schmidt, Harold-Edwin. 1973. "Personality correlates of the creative architecture student." *Perceptual and Motor Skills* 36:1030.

Schoenburg, R. 1972. "Strategies for meaningful comparisons." In Herbert Costner, ed., *Sociological Methodology.* San Francisco: Jossey-Bass.

Schuyler, Montgomery. 1964. *American Architecture and Other Writings.* New York: Atheneum.

Scott, Geoffrey. 1956. [1914]. *The Architecture of Humanism.* Garden City, N.Y.: Doubleday.

Scott, W. Richard. 1981. *Organizations.* Englewood Cliffs, N.J.: Prentice-Hall.

Scruton, Roger. 1979. *The Aesthetics of Architecture.* Princeton, N.J.: Princeton University Press.

Seeman, Melvin. 1967. "On the personal consequences of alienation in work." *American Sociological Review* 32:273–285.

Seitz, William. 1969. "Sculpture." In Louis Krohenberger, ed., *Quality: Its Image in the Arts.* New York: Atheneum.

Shapiro, Theda. 1976. *Painters and Politics.* New York: Elsevier.

Shawn, Ben. 1957. *The Shape of Content.* New York: Vintage.

Simmel, Georg. 1908. *Soziologie.* Leipzig: Dunker & Humblot.

Simmel, Georg. 1950. *The Sociology of Georg Simmel.* Translated and edited by Kurt H. Wolff. Glencoe, Ill.: Free Press.

Simmel, Georg. 1955. *Conflict and the Web of Group Affiliations.* Translated by Kurt H. Wolff and Reinhard Bendix. Glencoe, Ill.: Free Press.

Situationists. 1970. [1960]. "International Manifesto." In Ulrich Conrads, ed., *Programs and Manifestoes on 20th Century Art.* Cambridge: MIT Press.

Smigel, Erwin O. 1964. *The Wall Street Lawyer.* Glencoe, Ill.: Free Press.

Smith, Adam. 1937. *An Inquiry into the Nature and Causes of the Wealth of Nations.* New York: Random House.

Smith, C. Ray. 1977. *Supermannerism.* New York: E. P. Dutton.

Smith, P. F. 1974. *The Dynamics of Urbanism.* London: Hutchinson.

Sobel, Richard. 1978. "Is the big box on its way out?" *New Art Examiner* 6 (November):23.

Sommer, Robert. 1969. *Personal Space.* Englewood Cliffs, N.J.:Prentice-Hall.

Sontag, Susan. 1967. *Against Interpretation.* London: Eyre and Spottisworde.

Starbuck, William H. 1965. "Organizational growth and development." In James G. March, ed., *Handbook of Organizations.* Chicago: Rand McNally.

Steiner, Gary A. 1965. "Concluding remarks." In Gary A. Steiner, ed., *The Creative Organization*. Chicago: University of Chicago Press.

Stent, Gunther S. 1972. "Prematurity and uniqueness in scientific discovery." *Scientific American* 227 (December):84–95.

Sullivan, Louis. 1956. [1926]. *The Autobiography of an Idea*. New York: Press of the American Institute of Architects.

Summerson, John. 1963. *Heavenly Mansions and Other Essays on Architecture*. New York: W. W. Norton.

Tafuri, Manfredo. 1979. [1973]. *Architecture and Utopia*. Cambridge: MIT Press.

Tafuri, Manfredo. 1980. [1976]. *Theories and History of Architecture*. New York: Harper & Row.

Tannenbaum, Arnold S., Bogdan Karčič, Menachem Rosner, Mino Vianello, and Georg Wieser. 1974. *Hierarchy in Organizations*. San Francisco: Jossey-Bass.

Tatsuoka, Maurice M. 1971. *Multivariate Analysis*. New York: Wiley.

Taylor, Frederick W. 1911. *The Principles of Scientific Management*. New York: Harper & Row.

Taylor, Joshua. 1961. *Futurism*. New York: Museum of Modern Art.

Thompson, James D. 1967. *Organizations in Action*. New York: McGraw-Hill.

Thomson, Virgil. 1969. "Music." In Louise Kronenberger, ed., *Quality: Its Image in the Arts*. New York: Atheneum.

Tolbert, Charles M., Patrick Horan, and E. M. Beck. 1980. "The dual economy in American industrial structure." *American Journal of Sociology* 80:1095–1116.

U.S. Bureau of Labor Statistics. 1973, 1975, 1976. *Geographic Profile of Employment and Unemployment*. Washington, D.C.: Government Printing Office.

U.S. Bureau of the Census. 1974, 1976, 1977. *County Business Patterns*. Washington, D.C.: Government Printing Office.

Van der Meer, F. 1967. *Early Christian Art*. Translated by Peter Brown and Friedl Brown. New York: Faber and Faber.

Vázques, Adolfo Sanchez. 1973. *Art and Society*. New York: Monthly Review Press.

Venturi, Robert. 1966. *Complexity and Contradiction in Architecture*. Garden City, N.Y.: Doubleday.

Verba, Sydney. 1961. *Small Groups and Political Behavior*. Princeton: Princeton University Press.

Von Simpson, Otto. 1962. *The Gothic Cathedral*. Rev. ed. New York: Harper and Row.

Wachsmann, Konrad. 1975. [1957]. "Seven theses." In Ulrich Conrads, ed., *Programs and Manifestoes on 20th Century Architecture*. Cambridge: MIT Press.

Watkin, David. 1977. *Morality and Architecture*. Oxford: Oxford University Press.

Weber, Max. 1946. [1930]. *From Max Weber: Essays in Sociology.* Translated and edited by H. H. Gerth and C. Wright Mills. New York: Oxford University Press.

Weber, Max. 1976. *The Protestant Ethic and the Spirit of Capitalism.* Translated by Talcott Parsons with a new introduction by Anthony Giddens. London: Allen and Unwin.

Weinstein, B. 1977. "The demographics of politics of economic decline in New York City." *Annals of Regional Science* 11:65–73.

Westby, David L. 1960. "The career experience of the symphony musician." *Social Forces* 38:223–230.

White, Harrison C., and Cynthia White. 1965. *Canvases and Careers.* New York: Wiley.

White, Jerry. 1980. *Rothschild Buildings.* London: Routledge & Kegan Paul.

Whitehead, Alfred North. 1925. *Science and the Modern World.* New York: Macmillan.

Whitehead, Alfred North. 1978. *Process and Reality.* New York: Free Press.

Whyte, William H. 1968. *The Last Landscape.* New York: Doubleday.

Whyte, William H. 1980. *The Social Life of Small Urban Spaces.* New York: Municipal Art Society of New York.

Wilson, Aubrey. 1972. *The Marketing of Professional Services.* London: McGraw-Hill.

Wilson, James Q. 1966. "Innovation in organizations." In James D. Thompson, ed., *Approaches to Organizational Design.* Pittsburgh: University of Pittsburgh Press.

Wind, Edgar. 1969. [1963]. *Art and Anarchy.* New York: Vintage.

Winkelmann, D. 1973. "Trends in the design process." *Journal of the American Institute of Architects* 59 (February):13–20.

Winner, I. P. 1978. "Cultural semiotics and anthropology." In R. W. Bailey et al., eds., *The Sign.* Ann Arbor: University of Michigan Press.

Wolfe, Alan. 1977. *The Limits of Legitimacy.* New York: Free Press.

Wolfe, Tom. 1981. *From Bauhaus to Our House.* New York: Farrar Straus Giroux.

Wolff, Janet. 1983. *Aesthetics and the Sociology of Art.* London: George Allen & Unwin.

Wölfflin, Heinrich. 1963. *The Art of the Renaissance.* New York: Schocken.

Wotton, Sir Henry. 1961. [1624]. *The Elements of Architecture.* Charlottesville: University Press of Virginia.

Wright, Frank Lloyd. 1963. [1953]. *The Future of Architecture.* New York: Mentor Books.

Wright, Gwendolyn. 1981. *Building the Dream.* New York: Pantheon. MIT Press edition, 1983.

Zald, Mayer N. 1970. "Political economy." In Mayer N. Zald, ed., *Power in Organizations.* Nashville, Tenn.: Vanderbilt University Press.

Zaltman, Gerald, Robert Duncan, and Jonny Holbeck. 1973. *Innovations and Organizations.* New York: Wiley.

Zeisel, John. 1975. *Sociology and Architectural Design.* New York: Free Press.

Znaniecki, Florian. 1940. *The Social Role of the Man of Knowledge.* New York: Columbia University Press.

Zuckerman, Harriet. 1975. *Scientific Elites.* Chicago: University of Chicago Press.

Index